Beyond the Fragrance and Fun :
Chinese Tea-Wares and Tea Making Utensils
from the Wellington Wang Collection

國立歷史博物館
National Museum of History
中華文物保護協會

目　錄
CONTENTS

館長序

　　茶文化包含茶葉茶具的物質文明層面，以及豐厚的茶精神文化；中國和日本不僅細緻發展茶文化，亦滲透到生活中各層面，正所謂喝茶、品禪、玩壺、悟道。茶文化的風尚千年始終不衰，深入文學、藝術與社會生活，茶文化豐富了人類的精神生活，也促進陶瓷器、金銀器等工藝發展，本次展覽展出難得一見收藏精品，還有美不勝收的的百壺牆，對照中日茶文物，將是一場別具意義的文化盛會。

　　中日兩國自古以來就有著政治、經濟和文化的聯繫，茶文化是兩國源遠流長的文化交流結晶，尤以茶文化作為中日文化交流關係的紐帶，有特別重要的文化價值。中日茶文化都體現了天人合一的東方哲理。中國茶文化受到儒、道、佛的綜合影響，而日本茶道主要受佛教禪宗影響。在器物上，各自留下不同的美學發展痕跡。中國人是最先發現和利用茶的民族，世界各種語言中的「茶」，都是從中國對外貿易港口所在地廣東、福建等地「茶」的方言音譯轉變而來；中國人更有所謂「開門七件事，柴米油鹽醬醋茶」，表現生活習俗及飲食文化，強調了茶乃生活必需。日本室町幕府的中國文物收藏熱，以及全室塌塌米的室內起居設計，成為日本茶道的茶禮形成重要部分，本展規劃兩個不同文化體系，比較中日茶文化的同與異，以及兩方之間的交流互動。茶文化的傳承需要持續積澱，茶文化的發展則有賴於不斷的流動、創新。收藏家王度先生惠借多年收藏，使大眾有機會一窺中日兩國茶文化之美，至為可貴。

　　藉由文獻資料、茶具壺藝展示及茶文化情境展示，並將於展覽期間舉辦茶道示範教學，讓大眾瞭解茶與茶器在人文歷史方面密不可分的意義，期以展覽的形式與教育功能，提升國人生活品味及對文物藝術的欣賞境界，自是茶文化愛好者與研究者難得的交流機會。感謝王度先生為此展所付出的心力，也感謝李鳳山老師領導的梅門子弟共襄盛舉。相信這是一次別開生面並有積極意義的茶文化展覽。

國立歷史博物館　館長

黃永川

Preface

Besides the material aspects – tealeaves, tea-ware and tea-making utensils – tea culture also has a rich spiritual side to it. In both China and Japan, the art of making tea was developed to a very high level, and tea culture came to permeate every aspect of daily life; in particular, drinking tea was closely linked to both artistic appreciation and Buddhist self-cultivation. Tea has maintained its importance for well over a millennium, and has become deeply embedded in literature, arts, and ordinary life. Tea has enriched people's spiritual lives, and provided stimulus to the development of ceramics production, the manufacture of gold- and silverware and various other handicrafts. Visitors to this exhibition will be able to view precious and rarely seen artifacts relating to tea culture, including a magnificent wall-stand designed for displaying a large number of teapots simultaneously. The opportunity to compare tea culture artifacts from the Chinese and Japanese tea-making traditions gives the exhibition special significance.

Throughout history, there have been close political, economic and cultural ties between China and Japan, and tea culture can be thought of as the fruit of this long-standing process of cultural exchange. Tea culture has been one of the strands binding China and Japan together, a fact that gives it immense cultural value. In both China and Japan, tea culture was underlain by Eastern philosophy that emphasized the oneness of man and heaven. In China, tea culture reflected the combined influence of Confucian, Taoist and Buddhist thought, while in Japan the main spiritual influence on tea culture was Zen Buddhism. Significant differences can be seen in the aesthetic development of tea-ware in the two countries. The Chinese were the first people in the world to cultivate the tea plant and to begin drinking tea; in almost every language in the world, the word for "tea" derives from the name used in the Cantonese and Fukienese dialects of Chinese that were spoken in the Chinese ports from which tea was exported throughout the world. The Chinese saying "the seven things that are vital for daily existence are firewood, rice, vegetable oil, salt, soy sauce, vinegar and tea" reflects the importance of tea in daily life. In Japan, the development of the tea ceremony was heavily influenced by the vogue for collecting Chinese antiquities that developed during the Muromachi shogunate, and by Japanese house design, with its use of floor mats. This exhibition allows visitors to compare Chinese and Japanese tea-drinking culture, and to see how the two cultures influenced and interacted with one another. The development and dissemination of tea culture has been an ongoing process relying on constant change and innovation. This process can be seen in the items included in the exhibition (items which are the fruit of many years of collecting by Mr. Wellington Wang), enabling visitors to experience the beauty of Japanese and Chinese tea culture in one place.

The exhibition incorporates documentary materials, displays of tea-ware and tea-making utensils, and exhibits showing how tea culture developed over time. During the exhibition, special presentations will be held to instruct visitors in the rituals of tea making. The exhibition will help visitors to comprehend the immense significance that tea and tea-ware have held in the cultural history of East Asia. At the same time, the exhibition also constitutes a marvelous forum for the exchange of ideas between tea aficionados and researchers. Special thanks are due to Mr. Wellington Wang for all the time and effort that he has expended on the exhibition, and also to Mr. Li Feng-shan and his students. Thanks to them, it has been possible to create a tea culture exhibition that is truly groundbreaking, and that will make a positive contribution to the ongoing development of tea culture.

Director,
National Museum of History

序言

十八年前(1989)，同樣在國立歷史博物館，王度與同好推出「明清宜興壺藝精品展」。此舉不僅為茶具文化在台灣開啟了風氣，也為宜興茶壺在台灣市場首次掀起爭購競藏風潮。

一九九三前王度乘勝追擊，再度以「紫泥」鉅著問世，他的精闢論述與專業收藏，更持續牽動台灣收藏界如潮湧般地狂熱、沉溺於宜興茶壺。今天，王度累積其十八年來如癡如醉的收藏，再度借重國立歷史博物館舉辦了「鬥品鬪香—中日茶文化特展」。於公而言，對於喜愛茶文化的朋友，這毋寧是個天大的喜訊。於私來說，他於我，亦師、亦兄、亦友，興奮兼感佩之餘，當然不能不趁機說幾句話。

在文物團體的公益活動中，王度始終熱心奉獻、身先士卒。他曾任中華文物學會理事、海峽兩岸文化資產交流促進會副理事長、中華文物保護協會理事長。為支持、協助我的美夢，他也義不容辭擔任我所主持的雙清文教基金會董事。據我所知，沒有他的慷慨捐助，法務部調查局籌設的「煙毒博物館」恐將失色大半。王度，其實就是古道熱腸、急公好義的代名詞。

提起收藏文物，歷史絕對要給王度記上一筆。他愛物如染毒癮，看上的東西一定要據為己有，如今為了儲藏寶物居然「狡兔六窟」，除了住家塞滿文物幾無立足之地外，還另租了五間大房子藏滿他的心愛寶貝。收藏之廣、之多、之細，恐怕前無古人後無來者。他那種「雖千萬人吾往矣」的精神與毅力，正是我最敬仰之處。

此次茶具大展的內容，除了王度專精的紫砂壺之外，還兼容古今中外各俱其巧的茶具，爭奇鬥豔，目不暇給。王度年紀已逾耳順，可是他的思想與視野卻總是那麼年輕、活潑、有衝勁。這從他十八年來收藏生涯的變動、充實與多樣化中，不難略窺一二。

再說，每一個成功的男人背後，一定有個功不可沒的女人。王大嫂正是王度背後偉大的女性。王度愛買文物可說「揮霍無度、永不知足」，他常笑說：「我有心臟病和糖尿病，我太太說我還有神經病」。王大嫂雖然嘴巴這麼說，卻仍死心塌地、無怨無悔地在這個神經病背後，支持他、幫助他、跟隨他。這份一世真情，正是我和內人永遠尊敬、感動的。

適值「鬥品鬪香—中日茶文化特展」開幕之際，信手拈來，辭不達意。倘能為王度殫精竭慮、精心籌備的茶具大展略誌祝賀之意，並表彰他畢生忘情於文物的收藏與研究所付出的心力，則於願足矣！

雙清文教基金會 董事長

洪三雄

2007.08.10

Preface

It was 18 years ago in 1989 when Wellinton Wang and his friends put up the "Exhibition of the Art of Yixing Teapots of the Ming and Qing Dynasties," held at the National Museum of History. The exhibition set a trend in the teapot culture of Taiwan, while also creating a high demand for Yixing teapots in the local market.

In 1993, Wellinton Wang took advantage of the trend, this time with his zisha teapots. His writings and his impressive collection once again brought Yixing teapot collection to feverish heights in Taiwan. Today, he again presents his collection of 18 years ago at the National Museum of History through the "Fragrance of Appreciation: Tea Culture of China and Japan." Undoubtedly, this is a happy event for lovers of tea culture. Personally, I have to, as a student and as a friend, say a few words in the midst of all these excitements.

Wellinton Wang has always been a warm supporter of public welfare activities sponsored by artifact organizations. He was a director of the Chinese Artifacts Association, Vice-Chairman of the Bi-Coastal Cultural Assets Exchange Promotion Society and Chairman of the Chinese Artifacts Protection Association. To support and assist me in fulfilling my dream, he also readily accepted to become a director of the Shuangching Cultural and Educational Foundation, of which I am heading. I had been informed that without his generous support, the "Drug Museum" project of the Ministry of Justice would have lost half of its achievements. In all aspects of the description, Wellinton Wang is a passionate and generous supporter of all worthy causes.

Having mentioned artifact collecting, I tend to think Wellinton Wang deserves a name in history. He loves artifacts to the point of addiction and makes sure to obtain items that he has set his eyes on. Because of his growing collection, he has not only filled his house with his collection but also rented five large homes to house his treasures. The breadth, length and detail of his collection are unprecedented. It is this spirit and dedication that continue to amaze me.

The items of this exhibition include not just Wellinton Wang's zisha teapots but also cover tea utensils of many varieties from here and abroad, each competing in their eye-catching qualities. Although past the ripe age of 60, he is forever young, vibrant and dynamic in his ideas and visions. This is easy to see in the changes made, the improvements and the richer character of his 18-year-old teapot collection.

The adage goes that behind every man of success, there always is a woman. Wang's espouse is the woman behind all his success. We all know that Wellinton Wang is never satisfied in buying artifacts. "I have a heart disease and diabetes. My wife thinks I'm also mentally deranged," he often is heard saying. Although she says so, she has always given her full, unwavering support to this deranged man. This is something my wife and me will always find emulating.

My words fail me as I write these lines on the eve of the start of the "Fragrance of Appreciation: Tea Culture of China and Japan." Let me take this opportunity to congratulate him for a job well done in organizing this special exhibition and to act in testimony of his lifelong dedication to the study and collection of artifacts.

Mr. Steven Hung
President
Hung's Arts Foundation

自序

　　這次又展茶壺是有原因的，二十幾年前我曾第一個在台北舉辦個人茶壺收藏展。後來受邀在國立歷史博物館舉辦三人合展，一位已經不在了，他是鴻禧美術館創辦人張添根老先生，第二位是老朋友黃正雄先生，第三位就是我了。值得一提的是，當時我們三人的收藏還被選去印成郵票（共四件四張，我們三人一人一件，史博館的館藏一件）；這是中華民國郵票史上的首例。當時真轟動，因為台灣出產茶葉，好茶必用好壺沖泡，而透過這次展覽也帶動了全台灣收藏與觀賞宜興茶壺的風氣，宜興茶壺生產竟因此興盛起來；香港四大家為配合台灣的茶壺熱，每年都在香港舉辦茶壺展銷會，盛況空前，而台灣各縣市茶壺商人也游走海峽兩岸三地，幾乎到了全台總動員的程度，連我也要在三更半夜去搶購茶壺，更誇張的是我常跑機場接機，在機場就交易好了，現在想想真有點瘋狂。當時宜興每年都舉辦一次茶壺大展，我也親自趕去；講一個小故事，當時丁山最好的賓館房間連冰箱都沒有，我有糖尿病胰島素，一定要放冰箱，還好有一位工藝師家中有冰箱，我便放在他家中，他每天早上幫我送來，我現在想不起他是誰了，但我還是非常感激他。那時台灣喝茶、收壺的盛況可謂空前，宜興百分之九十的壺都賣到台灣，其紫砂廠從一廠擴充到五廠，風光一時，一把壺從十幾萬元炒到數百萬元，宜興工藝師買房子買車子，生活水平大為提升，很多工藝師在台灣都享有很高的知名度。

　　然而好景大概過了十幾年便不再了，當時全台做茶壺生意的有幾百家，現在就不知還有多少家？而宜興五廠也都相繼解散，改成各自經營，景況真是一落千丈！但幾位大名家的作品還是很搶手，好的東西是永遠不寂寞的，因為喝茶的人有增無減，好的茶壺永遠有人要買，要收藏。

　　這幾年來宜興工藝師及店家都同我聯絡，說台灣及宜興茶壺的興起，我是盡了一份心力，現在景氣卻到了谷底，王大哥你應該再帶頭把茶壺炒作一次救救大家。我想了一兩年，我覺得我應該再盡一份心力。憑良心講，紫砂茶壺真帶給我很多回憶及喜悅，所以我決定再辦一次茶具展，在國立歷史博物館黃館長的支持與同意下，我也開始行動，但我想紫砂壺我個人已展過好幾次了，在台灣類似的展覽也辦過幾百次了，再展紫砂壺未免有點單調；經過反覆思考，我覺得除了中國對茶壺重視外，日本茶道其實也很有特色，在世界上也是數一數二的，如果能把中日茶文化集合在一起展覽一定可以別開生面，同時對台灣茶文化的提倡也將是一項創舉！於是我便開始著手研究日本茶道，並積極收藏日本茶具。經過前後約兩年的全力衝刺，在許多同道朋友大力支持下，我收藏的日本茶具日益豐富與精緻，而我本人也逐漸由對日本茶具的收藏而逐漸進入到日本文化的領域。我覺得日本人在收藏文物方面真的很了不起，很值得我們學習。他們一個人力量不夠，便往往集合幾個人的力量來做，而且分工合作、巨細靡遺，不僅收藏的品類很完整，相關資料也非常周延，維護保養上更是望塵莫及；我們中國人這點就不同些了。這次為了讓日本人看看我們中國人在收藏文物方面的氣魄與品味，我是全力以赴，拼了！其間過程真的很辛苦，又覺得對不起我太太了，結婚四十三年來，我知道她對我很不滿意，但誰叫她要嫁給我呢？她說我有神經病，我也認了。其實我每一次收藏都包含著對我太太的一分歉意與深情，這是真的！

　　到此也說了不少，總之我想為台灣文化盡心盡力的意思是不變的。這次展覽得以順利舉辦，我首先要感謝國立歷史博物館黃永川館長和高玉珍副館長；其次是蘇啟明秘書，他本來是這次展覽的承辦人，後來因職務調動而離開展覽組，還好有戈思明主任、徐天福主任，及郭長江先生、溫玉珍小姐等鼎力協助；特別是溫玉珍小姐，她剛來史博館便承辦此項展覽，眞是有緣。此外李奇茂老師及周澄老師爲此次展覽所作的字畫、洪三雄老弟的序文、成耆仁博士及嵇若昕小姐的專文也都使展覽及這本圖錄增色不少。最後是好友蘇子非先生，感謝他在日本茶文物的蒐集上予我最大的支援、老友劉坤池先生對於中國茶文物的協助；還有負責展品攝影的于志暉及謝承佑兩位老弟以及翻譯的林渝珊小姐和協助整理文物的王錦川和陳銘基先生。我由衷感謝大家。

　　最後還是八個字：知足！惜福！感恩！捨得！

　　則於願足矣！

中華文物保護協會　榮譽理事長

Acknowledgments

There is a reason why this tea pot exhibition is being held again. Some twenty years ago, I was the first in Taipei to hold an exhibition on my tea pot collection. Later, I was invited to join two other collectors in holding a joint exhibition. Between the three of us: Mr. Tian-Gen Chang(張添根), the founder of the Chang's Foundation, has passed away and the other collector, Mr. Zhend-Xiong Huang(黃正雄), is an old friend of mine.

Something worth mentioning is that our collection, at that time, was chosen to be made into stamps. (A total of four stamps: one stamp per person and the 4th one was a collection from the National Museum of History). The collectable stamps were a hit back then, since it was a first in the history of the R.O.C. stamps.

Taiwan is famous for its tea manufacturing business, hence the saying a good teapot makes grest tea is well believed by the tea drinkers in Taiwan. For this reason, this particular joint exhibition pushed forward the climate of collecting and appreciating Yi-Xing(宜興)tea pots. Afterwards the tea manufacturing business flourished.

In order to comply with the great demand in tea pots, trade fairs were held in Hong Kong annually to satisfy the needs of its collectors. It was such an exceptionally grand occasion! Traders also travelled around China, Hong Kong and Taiwan to get the best tea pots. I even had to rush to places in the middle of the night to acquire tea pots. Many deals were made directly at the airport when I was there picking up potential dealers. Now thinking back, they were some fantastic times. Till this day, I still remember the days when Yi-Xing(宜興) had its annual shows.

Let me tell you a little story: The hotel I stayed at in Ding-Shan(丁山), which was the best at the time, did not have refrigerators. But since I am diabetic and needed insulin shots constantly, I had to store my insulin in the home of one of the craftsmen. The kind-hearted craftsman had to deliver my insulin shots every morning from his house to the hotel, although I don remember the name of the craftsman, I still wish to thank him for his kindness.

In those days, collecting and drinking tea were such a phenomenon that as much as 90% of the Yi-Xing(宜興) tea pots were sold to Taiwan. Zi-Sha(紫砂) factories were expanded from the initial one, to a later five. Prices of tea pots increased from a couple hundred thousand NT dollars to as much as a couple million NT dollars. It was a very glorious time. This phenomenon allowed the craftsmen to buy houses and cars and their life standard are well improved.

However, this glorious time did not last for more than a few years over a decade: from having more than a few hundred tea pot stores in Taiwan, to not knowing how many, or even if any, were left. Eventually all five Yi-Xing(宜興) factories had to be closed down. Everything just went downhill. Fortunately, though, works done by a few well known craftsmen were able to survive this recession. After all, great tea pots are still worth collecting.

I still kept in contact with the craftsmen and owners from the tea pot stores. Many came to me and asked me to think about recreating the tea pot phenomenon once more. I thought about what they had said over the next two years, and finally decided that I will give it a try and I will do my best to help.

To be honest with you, when I really think about it, Zi-Sha(紫砂) tea pots did bring me joy and happiness. So I decided to host the exhibition once more for old time sake. After receiving great support from Director Huang at the National Museum of History, I geared up and started preparing for the tea-ware and tea-making utensils exhibition. After careful consideration, I decided to add a new flavor to this eagerly awaited exhibition. Since Zi-Sha(紫砂) tea pots had been exhibited many times in the past, and hundreds of similar exhibitions had also been done through time, I thought about what could be done to make this one more special. After repeated consideration, I realized China is not the only place that puts a lot of emphasis on tea pots, Japan also does. Rituals of Japanese tea making are well known worldwide. So I thought to myself if we can have an exhibition on both Chinese and Japanese tea cultures, Not only would we be able to promote the tea culture in Taiwan, but this combination would also be a pioneer. Thus research and more collecting needed to be done.

After about two years of extensive study, I had not only collected tea-wares and tea-making utensils, I, had learned about the rituals of Japanese tea making. With the help of many friends of the same ideas, and careful learning, I was able to go beyond being simply a collector into someone who actually understands the aspects of the Japanese tea culture.

I admire the way the Japanese care for cultural and historical relics, there is still a lot for us to learn. The Japanese are well aware of the power of team work. Not only are their collections comprehensive, but the effort they have put into maintenance is extraordinary.

So much of my time was put into preparing this exhibition; I started to feel sorry for my wife. In our 43 years of marriage, I know she is not to crazy about many of my artifact collection, but what can I say？ she married me! She thinks I am crazy and I admit it. In fact every time I start a collection, it is incorporated with my sincere apology and deep love to my dear wife. Really, it is true!

In any case, my love for Taiwanese culture will never change. In order for this exhibition to proceed without a hitch, I have many people to thank. Above all, many thanks to director Yong-Chuan Huang(黃永川) and vice director Yu-Zhen Gao(高玉珍). Thanks to secretary Qi-Ming Su (蘇啓明), who was the promoter of this exhibition at the beginning, but ran away after he got a promotion! Therefore, special thanks to manager Si-Ming Ge(戈思明), manager Tian-Fu Hsu(徐天福), Mr. Chang-Jiang Guo(郭長江) and Ms. Yu-Chen Wen(溫玉珍). Especially Ms. Yu-Chen Wen(溫玉珍), this is her first exibition case after joining the National Museum of History. Also, thank you teacher Cheng Zhou(周澄) for the calligraphies and paintings you made specially for this exhibition. And thank you Mr. Steven-Hung(洪三雄) for your wonderfully written preface and Dr. Sung Kee In(成耆仁)Ms. Ruo-Xin Ji (嵇若昕)for the essays which had added colors to the booklet. Last but not least, many thanks to Mr. Zi-Fei Su(蘇志瑋), my dear friend and my biggest supporter; Mr. Kun-Chi Liu(劉坤池) for his assistance. Before I finish, I also wanted to thank Mr. Zhi-Hui Yu(于志暉) and Mr. Cheng-You Xie(謝承佑) for their great work and translator Miss Angie Lin(林渝珊). My sincere thanks to you all!

Finally, still these 8 characters:

知足! (contentment)

惜福! (be appreciate)

感恩! (show gratitude)

捨得! (willingness to give)

Wellington Tu Wang

2007.08

專文－鬥品團香－中日茶文化

白居易〈琵琶行〉與序－－

元和十年（815），予左遷九江郡司馬。明年秋，送客湓浦口。聞舟船中夜彈琵琶者，聽其音，錚錚然，有京都聲。問其人，本長安倡女，嘗學琵琶於穆曹二善才。年長色衰，委身為賈人婦。遂命酒，使快彈數曲。曲罷，憫然自敘少小時歡樂事；今漂淪憔悴，轉徙於江湖間。余出官二年，恬然自安，感斯人言，是夕始學有遷謫意，因為長句，歌以贈之。凡六百一十六言，命日：「琵琶行。」

潯陽江頭夜送客，楓葉荻花秋瑟瑟。主人下馬客在船，舉酒欲飲無管絃；醉不成歡慘將別，別時茫茫江浸月。

忽聞水上琵琶聲，主人忘歸客不發。尋聲闇問彈者誰？琵琶聲停欲語遲。移船相近邀相見，添酒迴燈重開宴。千呼萬喚始出來，猶抱琵琶半遮面。……大絃嘈嘈如急雨，小絃切切如私語。嘈嘈切切錯雜彈，大珠小珠落玉盤。……門前冷落車馬稀，老大嫁作商人婦。商人重利輕離別，前月浮梁買茶去。去來江口守空船，遶船月明江水寒。……

大家都知道：唐代陸羽（733-804）因著《茶經》（761），後世奉為茶神；《茶經》一書幾乎涵蓋了茶學的每一個層面。陸羽去世後十年左右，白居易寫下了〈琵琶行〉這首長歌，世人多為詩中琵琶女的身世與詩人的際遇掬一把同情淚，也總沈吟於「千呼萬喚使出來，猶抱琵琶半遮面」、「大珠小珠落玉盤」、「老大嫁作商人父」、「商人重利輕離別」等詩句中，低迴不能自已；於是往往忽略了琵琶女所嫁的商人離家，乃是為了前往江西浮梁「買茶」；這位商人原來是一位茶商！

唐代以前，國人飲茶風氣僅流行於長江流域的四川、兩湖、浙江、江蘇等產茶地帶，唐代以後遍及全國。由是之故，陸羽在八世紀中葉完成了《茶經》的撰寫，白居易〈琵琶行〉中所描繪的商人，則是一位前往浮梁買茶的茶商。

「茶」字在唐代以前寫作「荼」，唐玄宗開元二十三年（735）所頒示的字書《開元文字音義》中已作「茶」，陸羽《茶經》一書全作「茶」字。1953年，大陸考古工作人員在清理湖南長沙市望城縣石渚湖北岸的蘭岸嘴窯址時，採集到一個玉璧底圓口碗，碗心有墨書「荼?」二字，因此有學者認為這個碗或是一個早於《茶經》的「標準性茶具」。

根據封演的《封氏聞見記》（約成書於唐貞元年間，785-805）所敘：「茶，早采者為茶，晚采者為茗。本草云：止渴、令人少眠。南人好飲之，北人初不多飲。開元中，太山靈巖寺有降魔師大興禪教，學禪務於不寐，又不夕食，皆恃其飲茶。人自懷挾，到處煮飲，從此轉相仿效，遂成風俗。」由此可知，唐代飲茶風氣的普及，與禪宗的弘揚息息相關。陸羽本人與出家人的關係也十分密切，據說他本為棄兒，為湖北竟陵龍蓋寺智積禪師收養。智積禪師日常所飲的茶，總由陸羽親自烹煮，兩人名為師徒，實如父子。

唐代文人往往對佛學有所涉獵，文人雅士日常生活也總品茗。中唐以後，隨著飲茶風氣的興盛，茶事成為文人、禪僧競相吟詠的題材。騷人墨客飲茶，並非僅為解渴，更是一種心靈的洗滌與精神的放鬆，也是一種藝術情操的表現。風氣所及，遠渡重洋來到中國留學的日本遣唐使與遣唐僧也學得唐代文人與禪僧的茗飲活動。九世紀初，聞名古今的兩位日本留學僧　躓輭P最澄分別於回國時，行李中就帶著茶籽與碾茶的石臼等同行。這些學問僧回到日本國內，除了弘揚佛法，也推廣飲茶風尚。

宋代禪宗大盛，文人雅士對茶事的投入更盛前朝，此時來到宋境留學的日本僧人或士子也伴同關心茶事，浙江茶區的餘杭、臨安交界處的徑山寺是當時茶事的主要傳播地點。將徑山寺茶宴傳入日本者，主要有兩位日本高僧，一位是圓爾辨圜（1202年～1280年），另一位是南浦紹明；後者於南宋理宗開慶元年（1259）入宋，南宋度宗咸淳三年（1267）回國。

南宋理宗端平二年（1235，日本嘉禎元年），日本聖一國師圓爾辨圜從明州入宋，於淳祐元年（1241）回國。留學期間師從徑山寺三十四代住持無準法師。留學期間，圓爾辨圜除了鑽研佛理，還學習種茶、製茶技術，回國時將徑山寺裡以茶待客的泡茶、飲茶禮儀帶回日本。

大應禪師南浦紹明居停宋境前後九年，師從臨安府淨慈寺、徑山興聖萬壽寺住持　蛔i象山籍高僧虛堂智愚禪師。回國時，南浦紹明不僅帶去了徑山寺的茶種和種茶、製茶技術，同時傳去了供佛、待客、茶會、茶宴等飲茶習慣和儀式；虛堂智愚禪師還送他很多茶書、茶臺子等茶具。因此，日本史籍中關於宋代茶事的傳入，對於南浦紹明記載更多，例如日本《類聚名物考》記載：茶道之初，在正元中築前崇福寺開山，南浦紹明由宋傳入。又如日本的《本朝高僧傳》也說：南浦紹明由宋歸國，把茶臺子、茶道具一式帶到崇福寺。此外，《虛堂智愚禪師考》一書也載：南浦紹明從徑山把中國的茶臺子、茶典七部傳到日本；茶典中有《茶堂清規》三卷。

由於先有圓爾辨圜帶回的徑山寺茶宴禮儀，後有南浦紹明帶回的茶書與茶具，遂使日後日本發展出聞名遐邇的「茶道」文化。日本陶瓷界與好茶人士所推崇的黑釉天目碗，據了解起初也是當時日本禪僧從宋境帶回國的茶具。

唐宋兩代，中日兩國交流頻繁，文化上除了詩詞、儒學與佛學等的東傳，飲茶品茗也隨之東傳，同時隨之而往的就是當時的各式茶具。宋代以後，中日兩國的飲茶方式各自獨立發展，伴隨著的茶具也各自發展，各具特色。

唐宋兩代所飲之茶都是固形茶，唐人將喫茶、飲茶提升至精神文明的層面；宋人飲茶更講究茶品、火候、茶器、煮法、飲效；元代在飲茶文化的表現既不明顯，也不出色；明人放棄飲用末茶，改為沖泡芽茶（葉茶、散茶）為主，重視茶色、茶香、茶韻等，與今日喫茶法相去不遠。清代飲茶習尚與明代大致相同，但皇室與王公貴族在與蒙藏人士交往中，也加入飲用奶茶的行列，此為清代茶事與前朝不同之處。隨著飲茶方式的改變，所需之器用當然也隨之改變。但不論如何，中國人飲茶比較不拘形式，尤其明清以後，飲茶、品茗乃日常生活的一部份，更重自然，所謂形而上者為之道，形而下者謂之器矣！

唐宋兩代，日本承襲了中國喫茶風尚，進而融合其自身的生活習慣，遂視飲茶為一種修心養性、學習禮儀的生活規範，並發展出適於其民族性的「茶道」。其藉飲茶摒除雜念，為期藉假練真，故對飲茶環境的布置、器用的選擇都十分講求。日本茶屋必須幽雅清寂，屋內陳設井井有條，字畫古董排列有序，品茗時主客皆須正襟危坐，切合儀度地啜茗。

由於民族性的不同，中日人士飲茶態度遂截然不同，連帶在茶具的發展上，也分道揚鑣，各具特色！此次「鬥品團香－中日茶文化特展」展出中日兩國的茶器，並輔以相關器用，當能讓國人一窺其中異同，進而領略兩國民情之異同。

國立歷史博物館研究員

嵇若昕

Beyond the Fragrance and Fun : Tea Culture Of China and Japan(Condensed)

Suddenly the pipa sounds wafted in the air from a distant boat,
My guests have forgotten to leave and I knew not where we were.
Tracing the sound, we looked for the wonder maker.
The music stopped before we could utter a word.
We moved our boat near the musician's to invite
Here to drink at our feast replenished by lamplight.
We urged her over and again till she appeared,
With the pipa hiding half her face.

… The bold strings rattled like splatters of sudden rain,
The fine strings hummed like lovers' whispers.
Chattering and pattering, pattering and chattering,
Like pearls, large and small, on a jade plate falling.

… And the carriages at her door got fewer and fewer,
Till finally she had to lower herself marry a tea dealer.
All he thought of was money, parting was nothing to him,
The month before he'd gone to Fuliang, to buy tea,
And she had been left to tend the boat all alone,
Rowing it in the cold water under a full bright moon.

—Excerpts from Po Chu-i's Pipa Song

Lu Yu of the Tang Dynasty (733-804) is known as the Father of Tea for having written the "Tea Classic." This work covers almost every aspect of tea drinking. About 10 years after Lu died, Po Chu-i wrote his long poem "Pipa Song." Readers are often moved into compassion by the lady pipa player's story and her chance meeting with the poet. How they read with emotional baggage lines such as "We urged her over and again till she appeared, with the pipa hiding half her face" and "All he thought of was money, parting was nothing to him." Often, they forget that the trader to whom the pipa player was married was traveling to Fuliang in Jiangxi Province to buy tea. He was after all a trader of tea.

Before the Tang Dynasty, tea drinking was mainly concentrated along the shores of the Yangtze River, near Sichuan, Hunan, Hubei, Zhejiang, and Jiangsu where tea was traditionally grown. The practice of tea drinking eventually spread across China after the Tang Dynasty. This explains why Lu Yu completed his Tea Classic in the middle of the 8th Century, and that the trader mentioned in Po Chu-i's Pipa Song was a tea merchant who went to Fuliang on business.

Tea was written as a different character before the Tang Dynasty. In his Tea Classic, Lu Yu used the character we currently use. The spread of tea drinking in the Tang Dynasty was closely related to the propagation of Zen Buddhism. Lu himself shared close relationships with monks. Legends have it that he was an abandoned child and was adopted by Master Zhiji of Lunggai Temple in Hubei's Jingling. It is said that Lu Yu personally brewed tea for Master Zhiji on a daily basis. Although formally seen as master and disciple, the two shared a father and son relationship.

The Tang literati often dabbled in Buddhism. They were drinkers of tea in their daily lives. After the middle of the Tang Dynasty, as tea drinking became more prominent, the practice also became a theme for poetic creations among the literati and Zen monks alike. Tea was not just taken as a thirst-quencher. It is also a means for spiritual cleansing and relaxation, as well as an expression of artistic sentiments. The art of tea became so widespread that Japanese envoys and monks sent to Tang China for studies also picked up the practice from the Tang men of learning and monks. At the beginning of the 9th Century, the two famous Japanese scholar monks—Kukai and Saicho—returned to Japan where they spread the art of tea drinking.

By the Song Dynasty, the popularity of tea grew even more, thanks to a rise in Zen Buddhism and the continued dedication of the literati. The Japanese scholars and monks who came to China at this period in history also sought for learning on the art of tea. Jingshan Temple, located between the borders of Yukeng and Linan in Zhekiang Province's tea planting zone, was then the major source spring for the propagation of tea art.

Exchanges between China and Japan were frequent during the Tang and Song Dynasties. In terms of culture, there was a transmission of poetry, Confucianism and Buddhism to Japan, through which the art of tea drinking also followed suit, including the tools of the art. After the Song Dynasty, the art of tea drinking developed independently in China and in Japan, as well as in their specialties and brewing paraphernalia. As the method of tea preparation and drinking evolved, the tools used also changed with them. The Chinese drank tea in a less formal way, especially after the Ming and Qing Dynasties. It became a part of daily life and as such, paid attention to naturalness.

The Japanese absorbed the Chinese art of tea drinking in the Tang and Song Dynasties. They added their own life styles into the art, which took on characteristics more related to personal cultivation, rituals and regulation of life. For this, they developed "chado," the tea ceremony that suits the Japanese people's character best. Through the act of tea drinking, chado was a way to attain inner concentration. It paid meticulous attention to the venues and tools for drinking tea. Teahouses have to be serene and elegant in atmosphere, with the interior arranged neatly, and decorated with painting and calligraphy scrolls, antiques, etc. During the ceremony, participants don formal attires and kneel down as they imbibe tea with great decorum.

Folk characteristics led to the stark difference in the tea drinking cultures of China and Japan. Similarly, their tools also developed in different ways. This exhibition, entitled *The Fragrance of Appreciation: Tea Culture of China and Japan*, features tea drinking paraphernalia in China and Japan. It is a chance for locals to view and compare the differences between the tea cultures of the two countries.

Ruo-Xin Ji
Researcher, National Palace Mu-
seum

書畫　江兆申

H：61cm　W：35.5cm

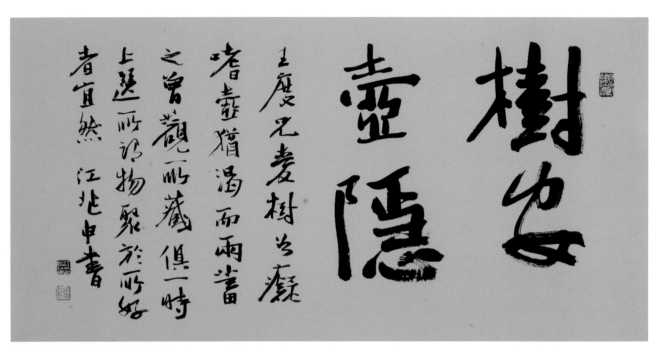

書法　江兆申

H：67.5cm　W：35cm

水墨山水　周澄　2007 年作

H：137cm　W：69cm

水墨茶壺　任伯年

H：37cm　W：27.5cm

漢字石刻　　　**TP-593**	漢字石刻　　　**TP-594**	漢字石刻　　　**TP-595**
印文：泉	印文：喫茶去	印文：茶
作者：李鎮成	作者：李鎮成	作者：李鎮成
材質：巴林石	材質：巴林石	材質：巴林石
Ink stone	Ink stone	Ink stone
H：5.6cm　W：8.2cm	H：6.3cm　W：9cm	H：12cm　W：10cm

圖　版 Plates

吉祥紫砂壺（沉船）　　**TP-014**

Zisha teapot found from sunken ship

H：15cm　　W：21.3cm

　　在沉船發生的年代，西方對中國瓷器的需求量極大。自唐代以來中國的瓷器就大量外銷，在波斯、中東、東南亞和歐洲到處都可以見到中國的瓷器。特別是到了宋元以後，很多歐洲商人專程來中國訂燒瓷器運返家鄉銷售，因此很多中國瓷器都帶有歐洲風格。一般來說中國外銷瓷經常用兩條海運路線，分為東、西兩線。東線從福建泉州、閩南沿海出發，經臺灣、菲律賓、馬古魯海峽到印尼，再將瓷器運至歐洲。西線是自廣州開始，沿海南島到越南峴港，經越南海岸線到馬來西亞過麻六甲海峽到印尼爪哇。

　　180 年前的中國，已因鴉片的大量輸入而使經濟開始崩潰。西元 1822 年這艘當時中國最大型的木製三桅帆船「德昇號」（The Tek Sing），從中國廈門駛往古稱爪哇的印尼。船上滿載著兩千餘人離開家國，當中大多是預備到爪哇的甘蔗園裡尋求生路的苦力，或是一些遠赴南洋販售各種中國特產和珍奇物品的商人。當船駛到蘇門答臘和爪哇島之間的海面上時，船體觸礁並迅即沉沒，當時船上只有 198 人僥倖獲救，死難者人數是有史以來海難中死亡人數最多的，這次船難被後人喻為「東方鐵達尼號」（Titanic of the East）。這艘沉船在多年後被打撈出多達 35 萬件中國瓷器，甚至還有明末清初製壺名家惠孟臣所製的珍貴宜興壺。這是世界陶瓷考古及貿易史上的一次重大發現，由於這些壺具曾長眠於海底，壺身氧化斑剝的情形，正可供研究參考之用。

吉祥紫砂壺（沉船）　**TP-013**

Zisha teapot found from sunken ship

H：14.8cm　W：21.3cm

圓燈紫砂壺（沉船）　　**TP-015**

Round shaped zisha teapot found from sunken ship

H：13cm　W：20.2cm

圓燈紫砂壺（沉船）　**TP-003**

Round shaped zisha teapot found from sunken ship

H：11.2cm　W：15cm

梨形紫砂壺（沉船）　詩句孟臣款　**TP-017**

Pear shaped zisha teapot with Mengchen's signature
and poetic inscribtion found from sunken ship

H：8.2cm　W：15cm

文旦朱泥壺（沉船）　**TP-007**

Pomelo shaped red clay teapot found from sunken ship

H：10.7cm　W：16.2cm

文旦朱泥壺（沉船）　**TP-011**

Pomelo shaped red clay teapot found from sunken ship

H：10.5cm　W：16.5cm

文旦朱泥壺（沉船） **TP-012**

Pomelo shaped red clay teapot found from sunken ship

H：10.8cm　W：15.7cm

文旦朱泥壺（沉船） **TP-006**

Pomelo shaped red clay teapot found from sunken ship

H：10.5cm　W：16cm

蓮子朱泥壺（沉船）　　**TP-010**

Red clay teapot found from sunken ship

H：10.8cm　W：15.7cm

蓮子朱泥壺（沉船）　**TP-008**

Red clay teapot found from sunken ship

H：8.2cm　W：12cm

扁燈朱泥壺 (沉船)　**TP-002**

Compressed red clay teapot found from sunken ship

H：6cm　W：14cm

扁燈朱泥壺(沉船) **TP-016**

Compressed red clay teapot found from sunken ship

H：6.3cm　W：14cm

梨形朱泥壺（沉船） TP-001

Pear shaped red clay teapot found from sunken ship

H：9.8cm　W：17cm

直筒朱泥壺（沉船）　詩句孟臣款　　**TP-005**

Cylindrical red clay teapot with Mengchen's signature
and poetic inscription found from sunken ship

H：9.8cm　W：12cm

直筒朱泥壺（沉船）　詩句孟臣款　　**TP-004**

Cylindrical red clay teapot with Mengchen's signature
and poetic inscription found from sunken ship

H：9.8cm　W：12.5cm

綴球朱泥壺 (沉船)　**TP-009**

Red clay teapot found from sunken ship

H：9.5cm　W：13.6cm

水仙花綾瓣紫砂壺　墨林堂大彬款　　**TP-149**

Zisha teapot with narcissus design

H：9cm　W：18.5cm

23

博浪鎚紫砂壺　陳鳴遠款　**TP-127**
Zisha teapot with a chian shot design
H：8cm　W：11cm

水仙花六方黃泥壺　鳴遠款　**TP-053**

Hexagonal yellow clay teapot with narcissus design

H：8cm　W：14.5cm

獅鈕圓珠紫砂大壺　　**TP-080**

Large round shaped zisha teapot with lion knob

H：20cm　W：26.5cm

梅幹圓珠紫砂壺　仲美款　**TP-109**

Round Zisha teapot with marked

H：12cm　W：19.5cm

腰帶四方紫砂壺　陳秉文製款　**TP-081**

Square zisha teapot in shape of waist belt

H：16cm　W：22.5cm

錢鈕圓珠紫砂大壺　用卿款　　**TP-079**

Large round shaped zisha teapot with coin knob

H：17.3cm　W：29cm

蓮子醬釉紫砂壺　　**TP-096**

Brown colored glaze zisha teapot

H：16.5cm　W：32cm

六方菱形紫砂壺　　**TP-100**

Hexagonal diamond shaped zisha teapot

H：15cm　W：22cm

四方開光紫砂壺　徐顯名制款　**TP-076**
Square zisha teapot with mark
H：19.5cm　W：26.5cm

吉祥紫砂直流壺　邵正來制　**TP-125**

Cylindrial Zisha teapot with mark

H：11.5cm　W：16cm

甕形紫砂壺　　邵春元制款　　**TP-082**

Jug shaped zisha teapot with mark

H：15cm　　W：20cm

鼓腹紫砂提樑壺　邵元祥制款　　**TP-075**

Compressed zisha teapot with overhead handle

H：20.5cm　W：27cm

吉祥紫砂大壺　荊溪邵元祥制款　　**TP-512**

Zisha teapot with mark

H：21cm　W：32.5cm

吉祥紫砂大壺　荊溪邵元祥制款　**TP-164**

Large zisha teapot with mark

H：21cm　W：31.5cm

吉祥紫砂大壺　荆溪邵元祥制款　**TP-073**

Large zisha teapot with mark

H：23cm　W：35cm

山水彩竹節紫砂大壺　漢珍款 **TP-337**

Large Zisha teapot with bamboo section and landscape design with mark

H：15.5cm　W：22.5cm

半彩四方開光紫砂壺　　**TP-097**

Square zisha teapot in enamel colors

H：15.5cm　　W：20cm

吉祥滿彩紫砂大壺　邵元祥制款　　　**TP-074**

Large zisha teapot with famille rose enamel colors with mark

H：21cm　W：32.5cm

全彩紫砂壺　邵形然制　**TP-375**

Zisha teapot in enamel colors with mark

H：17.5cm　W：27.5cm

半彩斜角漢方紫砂壺　澹然齋　　**TP-369**

Han style zisha teapot in enamel colors with mark

H：20cm　W：21.5cm

滿彩四方紫砂壺　　**TP-093**

Square zisha teapot in enamel colors

H：17.5cm　　W：21.5cm

山水彩吉祥紫砂壺　　**TP-370**

Zisha teapot with landscape design in enamel colors

H：19cm　　W：30cm

爐均釉漢方紫砂壺　**TP-268**

Zisha teapot with Robbin's egg glaze of the Han style

H：20cm　W：19.5cm

綠釉漢方紫砂壺　陽羨蚨器款　**TP-364**

Green glaze zisha teapot in Han style with mark

H：19cm　W：19cm

堆泥漢方紫砂壺　　TP-500

Zisha teapot in applique design of Han style

H：19.5cm　W：21cm

漢方紫砂壺　　TP-501

Zisha teapot of Han style

H：19cm　W：21.5cm

牟彩漢方紫砂壺　　**TP-246**

Zisha teapot with blue enamel colors of Han style

H：18cm　W：18cm

粉彩雲角漢方紫砂壺　　**TP-499**

Zisha teapot in famille rose enamel colors of Han style

H：19.5cm　W：21cm

六方描金紫砂壺　　董永年製款　　**TP-168**

Hexagonal gold brushed zisha teapot with mark

H：11.5cm　W：17cm

四方描金紫砂壺　　董永年製款　　**TP-171**

Gold brushed zisha teapot with mark

H：14cm　W：18cm

蓮子黃砂壺　　**TP-095**

Yellow clay teapot

H：8cm　　W：17.5cm

斗笠式紫砂壺　　**TP-536**

Leaf hat shaped zisha teapot

H：13cm　　W：14.5cm

描金紫砂壺　朗岭製款　**TP-085**

Gold brushed zisha teapot with mark

H：6.7cm　W：15cm

描金圓珠紫砂壺　清德堂款　**TP-107**

Gold brushed zisha teapot with mark

H：9cm　W：16.5cm

菊花八辦紫砂壺　楊秀初款　**TP-316**

Chrysanthemum petal shaped zisha teapot with mark

H：10cm　W：16.5cm

圓珠菊瓣紫砂壺　楊彭年製款　**TP-518**

Round chrysanthemum petal shaped zisha teapot with mark

H：10cm　W：16cm

藍彩子母紫砂壺　TP-340

Two connected zisha teapot in blue enamel color

H：11cm　W：16cm

藍彩紫砂壺　鄧奎款　TP-084

Zisha teapot in blue enamel color with mark

H：11.5cm　W：15.5cm

獅扭圓珠線條紫砂壺　**TP-519**

Zisha teapot with lion knob

H：10cm　W：16.5cm

古蓮子紫砂壺　萬泉款　**TP-187**

Zisha teapot with mark

H：9.5cm　W：15.5cm

堆泥半圓紫砂壺　**TP-537**

Zisha teapot in applique design

H：8cm　W：16.5cm

堆泥綾瓣蓮子紫砂壺　邵玉亭製款　**TP-150**

Zisha teapot in applique design with mark

H：13cm　W：16cm

博浪鎚紫砂壺　東石款　　**TP-135**

Zisha teapot with a chian shot design with mark

H：9cm　W：11cm

博浪鎚紫砂壺　東石款　　**TP-129**

Zisha teapot with a chian shot design with mark

H：10cm　W：12.5cm

三足圓扁紫砂壺　陽羨王東石製款　　**TP-224**

Oblate shaped zisha teapot with tree legged with mark

H：6cm　W：14cm

57

鉞蓋紫砂壺　心舟款　　**TP-511**

Zisha teapot with mark

H：6cm　　W：10.5cm

鼓形段泥壺　曼陀華館款　　**TP-508**

Round blended clay teapot with mark

H：7.5cm　　W：13cm

樹癭黃泥壺 **TP-377**

Tree knur shaped yellow clay teapot

H：10cm　W：17cm

獅扭圓珠黃泥壺 **TP-379**

Round shaped yellow clay teapot with lion knob

H：11.5cm　W：18.5cm

井欄黃泥壺　玉成窯造　　**TP-204**

Yellow clay teapot with mark

H：7.5cm　W：16cm

葫瓜式段泥壺　浙甯玉成窯造款　**TP-522**

Calabash shaped blend clay teapot with mark

H：11.5cm　W：14.5cm

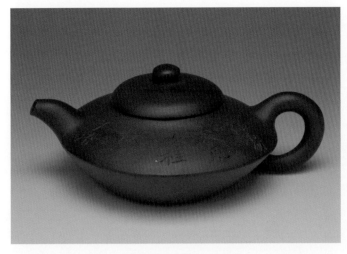

合歡紫砂壺　陽羨挺來式製　**TP-587**

Zisha teapot with mark

H：5.5cm　W：13cm

平蓋刻字圓扁紫砂壺　林園款　**TP-331**

Oblate zisha teapot with lid inscribed Chinese character with mark

H：6.5cm　W：12.5cm

漢磚堆泥黃泥壺　茶熟香溫款　**TP-116**

Brick shaped yellow clay teapot of applique designed with mark

H：15cm　W：14cm

斜角圓扁紫砂壺　茶熟香溫款　**TP-313**

Compressed zisha teapot with mark

H：8cm　W：17cm

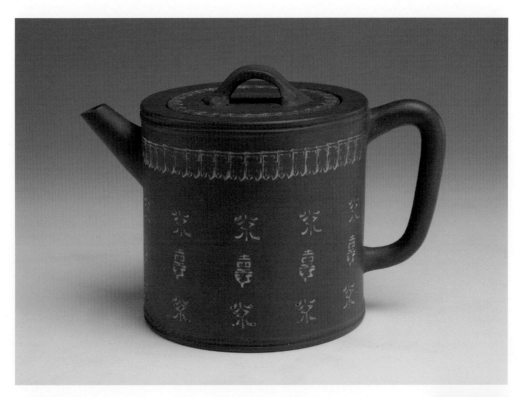

直筒印花紫砂壺　符生鄧奎監造款　**TP-118**

Cylindrical zisha teapot with stamped pattern with mark

H：10cm　W：14cm

四方泥繪紫砂壺　**TP-115**

Painted zisha teapot in square shape

H：9.5cm　W：14cm

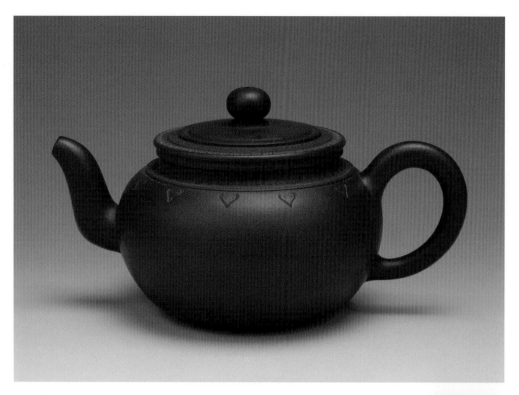

圓珠紫砂壺　榮祥款　**TP-213**

Zisha teapot with mark

H：9cm　W：17cm

蓮花碗形朱泥壺　**TP-192**

Lotus shaped red clay teapot

H：10cm　W：13.5cm

笠形紫砂壺　阿曼陀室　　**TP-061**

Pearl shaped zisha teapot with mark

H：7.5cm　W：13.5cm

井欄紫砂壺　阿曼陀室　**TP-120**

Zisha teapot inscribed with Chinese character

H：7cm　W：15cm

古錢半月紫砂壺　**TP-181**

Half moon shaped zisha teapot with coin shaped knob

H：6cm　W：17.5cm

半彩梅椿紫砂壺　**TP-136**

Zisha teapot in the form of a plum tree trunk
and enamel colors with mark

H：9.5cm　W：18cm

四方藍釉紫砂壺　宜興紫砂茗壺　**TP-269**

Square zisha teapot in blue glaze with mark

H：14cm　W：17cm

三足堆泥紫砂提樑壺　**TP-530**

Three legged zisha teapot in applique design with overhead handle

H：16.5cm　W：16.5cm

菊瓣紫砂提樑壺　　**TP-070**

Zisha chrysanthemum petal shaped teapot with overhead handle

H：16cm　W：16cm

四方隱角高竹黃泥壺　**TP-543**

Square yellow clay teapot

H：10cm　W：13cm

四方隱角竹紫砂壺　**寶珍款**　**TP-153**

Square zisha teapot of bamboo section handle with mark

H：13cm　W：17cm

居士紫砂壺　**TP-147**

Zisha teapot with figures

H：8.5cm　W：15cm

壽翁貼花紫砂壺　**TP-296**

Zisha teapot in applique design

H：21.5cm　W：23.5cm

四方斜角紫砂壺　石林中入款　**TP-252**

Square zisha teapot with mark

H：18cm　W：17.5cm

嵌金間線碗形紫砂壺　**TP-391**

Gold inlaid bowl shaped zisha teapot

H：13cm　W：16cm

高蓮子紫砂壺　**TP-179**

Zisha teapot

H：12cm　W：15cm

橋扭桶鋪砂紫砂壺　時大彬製款　**TP-502**

Cylindrical Zisha teapot of arch shaped knob with mark

橋扭紫砂壺　時大彬制款　　**TP-363**

Cylindrical zisha teapot of bridge shape knob with mark

H：17cm　W：18.5cm

太極八卦紫砂壺　大文款　**TP-087**

Zisha teapot with eight trigrams design

H：9.5cm　W：16cm

雙線圓竹紫砂壺　桂林款　**TP-111**

Zisha teapot with bamboo section design

H：13.5cm　W：22.5cm

漢君綠泥壺　窓齋款　**TP-185**

Green glaze teapot

H：8cm　W：17.5cm

圓扁紫砂提樑壺　松壺道人款　**TP-089**

Oblate shaped zisha teapot of overhead handle with mark

H：14.7cm　W：16cm

包袱紫砂提樑壺　任佰年款　**TP-101**

Zisha teapot in the shape of a wrapped cloth with mark

H：13.5cm　W：12cm

竹段黃泥提樑壺　**TP-541**

Yellow clay teapot with bamboo section design and overhead handle

H：17.5cm　W：15.5cm

臥獅紫砂壺　　第一獅球款　**TP-110**

Zisha teapot of lion knob with mark

H：12cm　W：21.5cm

柿子紫砂壺　　金壽款　**TP-105**

Persimmon shaped zisha teapot with mark

H：10cm　W：20.5cm

砲管紫砂壺　**TP-394**

Zisha teapot

H：12cm　W：16.5cm

葵花形紫砂壺　**TP-193**

Sunflower shaped zisha teapot

H：10.5cm　W：18.5cm

井欄腰線紫砂壺　蜀山名壺友蘭款　TP-128

Cylindrical zisha teapot with mark

H：11.5cm　W：16.5cm

鐘式腰線紫砂壺　TP-521

Zisha teapot in shape of a bell

H：9cm　W：14.5cm

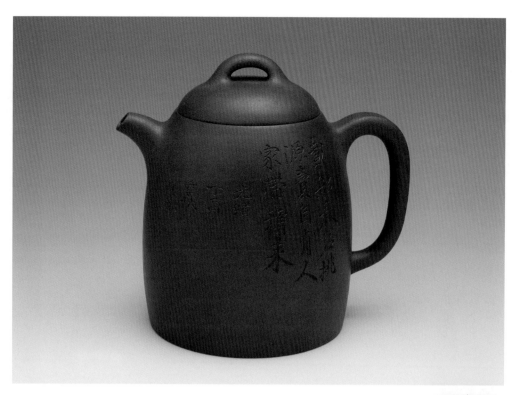

秦權紫砂壺　林園款　**TP-069**

Measuring weight shaped zisha teapot marked by Lin Yuan

H：12.5cm　W：13.5cm

南瓜紫砂壺　林園款　**TP-054**

Pumpkin shaped zisha teapot marked by Lin Yuan

H：8.5cm　W：14cm

梅段紫砂壺 **TP-517**

Plum tree trunk shaped zisha teapot

H：9.5cm　W：18cm

百果紫砂壺 **TP-568**

Zisha teapot

H：8.7cm　W：11.8cm

長方紫砂扁壺　陳共之制　**TP-189**

Compressed zisha teapot with marked

H：7cm　W：15cm

鏡瓦紫砂壺　少峰款　**TP-134**

Zisha teapot with marked

H：7.5cm　W：17.5cm

扁腹紫砂壺　玉和齋款　**TP-152**

Compressed zisha teapot with mark

H：9cm　　W：17.5cm

橋鈕圓扁紫砂壺　　　　**TP-520**

Oblate shaped zisha teapot with bridge knob

H：8cm　　W：15cm

橋鈕線圓紫砂壺　**TP-395**

Zisha teapot with arch shape knob

H：8.5cm　W：18.5cm

三足圓扁紫砂壺　郝記大亨款　**TP-212**

Three legged oblate shaped zisha teapot with mark

H：8cm　W：17.5cm

巴拿馬綴球紫砂壺　壽珍款　**TP-098**

Zisha teapot with mark

H：12.5cm　W：16.5cm

黃泥保溫茶具組　冰心道人款　**TP-498**

A set of yellow clay teapot and warmer with mark

H：13cm　W：14cm（左）

葵瓣腰線紫砂壺　　**TP-217**

Sunflower petal shaped zisha teapot with waist line design

H：8.5cm　W：16.5cm

水仙花瓣紫砂壺　　**TP-220**

Narcissus petal shaped zisha teapot

H：9cm　W：18cm

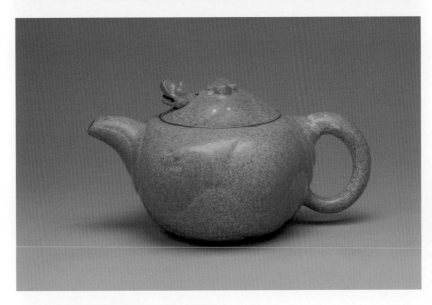

魚化龍紫砂壺　　**TP-270**

Zisha teapots with a fish transforming into a dragon design

L19.5cm　　H11cm

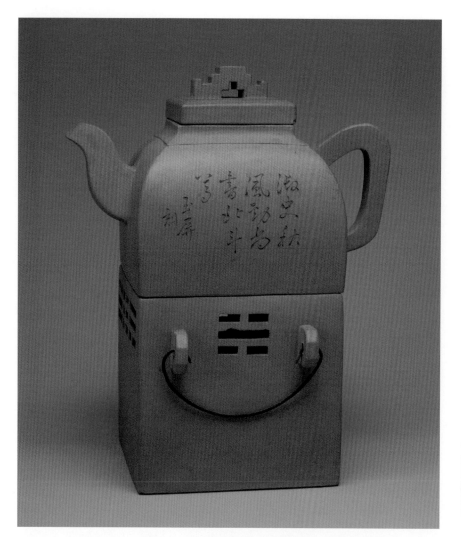

兩截式四方城塔黃泥壺　淦成鐵畫軒製款　TP-367

A set of square yellow clay teapot and warmer

H：23cm　W：19cm

六方碗形紫砂壺　**TP-523**

Hexagonal bowl shaped zisha teapot

H：9.5cm　W：18cm

兩截式紫砂壺　**TP-343**

A set of zisha teapot and cup

H：11.5cm　W：17.5cm

井欄紫砂壺　**TP-311**

Zisha teapot

H：9cm　W：15cm

堆泥四方斜角紫砂壺　**TP-200**

Square zisha teapot with stamped pattern in applique design

H：12cm　W：17.5cm

樹椿紫砂壺　供春款　**TP-078**

Zisha teapot in the form of tree trunk with mark

H：15cm　W：22cm

樹椿黃泥壺　平定陶業公司款　**TP-114**

Red clay teapot in the form of tree trunk with mark

H：12cm　W：19cm

松幹椿紫砂壺　TP-202

Pine trunk shaped zisha teapot

H：9.5cm　W：18cm

蝙蝠桃把紫砂壺　TP-529

Zisha teapot with bats

H：9.5cm　W：17cm

吉祥紫砂壺　　**TP-390**

Zisha teapot

H：11cm　W：15cm

酒壺式紫砂壺　　**TP-194**

Vessel shaped zisha teapot

H：15cm　W：13.5cm

石瓢紫砂壺　**TP-144**

Stone weight shaped zisha teapot

H：8.5cm　W：16.5cm

漢鐘式黃泥壺　**TP-221**

Bell shaped yellow clay teapot

H：11cm　W：17cm

圓珠朱泥壺　**TP-567**

Round shaped zisha teapot

H：8.5cm　W：13.5cm

橋扭山水紫砂壺　**TP-397**

Zisha teapot with landscape design and arch shape knob

H：13cm　W：21.5cm

葫蘆流西施紫砂壺　阿亮款　**TP-342**

Calabash shaped zisha teapot with mark

H：6cm　W：12.5cm

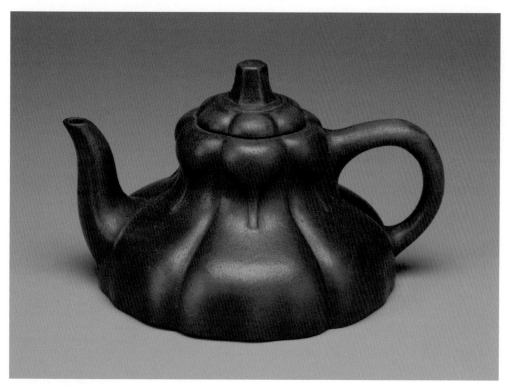

水仙花瓣紫砂壺　**TP-540**

Narcissus petal shaped zisha teapot with mark

H：8.5cm　W：13cm

藍彩圓扁紫砂壺　**TP-376**

Oblate shaped zisha teapot with blue enamel color

H：5.5cm　W：13cm

粉彩獅扭紫砂壺　**TP-258**

Zisha teapot with famille rose enamel color and lion knob

H：10cm　W：19cm

橋鈕鐘式紫砂壺　TP-515

Bell shaped teapot with arch shape knob

H：10.5cm　W：18cm

紫砂壺　TP-590

Zisha teapot

H：13.5cm　W：16.5cm

牛蓋紫砂壺　　**TP-516**

Zisha teapot

H：8cm　W：19cm

扁腹仿古紫砂壺　　**TP-396**

Zisha teapot

H：11cm　W：19cm

印花扁圓陶壺　　**TP-137**

Oblate shaped clay teapot

H：11cm　W：17cm

圓竹段泥茶具組　　**TP-621**

A set of teapot in bamboo trunk design

H：10cm　W：18.5cm（茶壺）

（左）洋桶紫砂壺 （右）刻詩句保溫壺　　**TP-428**

L : Cylindrical zisha teapot　　R : Teapot warmer inscribed with poem

H：27cm　W：20cm

甕形洋筒墨泥壺　豫豐款　　**TP-249**

Teapot in black glaze with mark

H：18cm　W：24.5cm

洋筒提樑紫砂壺　何道洪印　　**TP-250**

Zisha teapot with overhead handle with mark

H：15cm　W：16.5cm

洋筒提樑紫砂壺　　**TP-238**

Zisha teapot with overhead handle

H：24.5cm　W：26.5cm

洋筒提樑紫砂壺　　**TP-237**

Zisha teapot with overhead handle

H：23cm　W：26.5cm

洋筒提樑紫砂壺　**TP-092**

Zisha teapot with overhead handle

H：21.5cm　W：26.5cm

鼓腹紫砂提樑壺　壽款　**TP-373**

Compressed zisha teapot with overhead handle marked with "Zho"

H：11.5cm　W：22.5cm

洋筒提樑紫砂壺　友廷款　**TP-374**

Cylindrical Zisha teapot with overhead handle

H：14cm　W：18cm

粉彩提樑紫砂壺　TP-247

Zisha teapot with famille rose colors and overhead handle

H：14cm　W：17cm

錫制洋筒提樑壺　TP-248

Pewter teapot with overhead handle

H：17.5cm　W：24cm

圓珠錫包紫砂提樑壺　　**TP-254**

Zisha teapot encased in pewter with overhead handle

H：10cm　　W：17.5cm

酒桶形錫包紫砂提樑壺　　**TP-251**

Cask shaped Zisha teapot encased in pewter with overhead handle

H：16.5cm　　W：19cm

TP-253

三足嵌銀提樑墨泥壺
邵景南款
Silver inlaid three legged black clay
teapot with overhead handle
H：16.5cm　W：18.5cm

加彩錫包紫砂提樑壺　王南林制　　**TP-372**

Zisha teapot encased in pewter with enamel colors and overhead handle
H：14cm　W：20cm

龍旦朱砂壺　大彬製款　　**TP-143**

Egg shaped red clay teapot with mark

H：10.5cm　W：12.5cm

大口嘴文旦朱砂壺　**TP-140**

Pomelo shaped red clay teapot

H：8cm　W：13cm

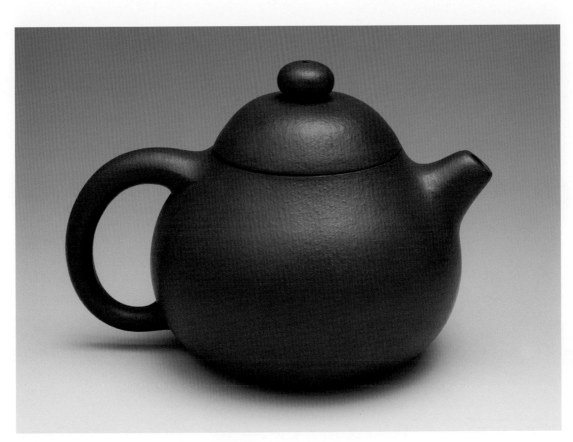

文旦朱泥壺　詩句款　**TP-067**

Pomelo shaped red clay teapot with poetic inscribtion mark

H：11cm　W：15cm

TP-113

六方貼花朱泥黃

Hexagonal red clay teapot
with applique design

H：15cm　W：13.5cm

110

五方獸扭紫砂壺　　**TP-317**

Pentagonal zisha teapot with animal knob

H：8.5cm　　W：13cm

四方貼花朱砂壺　　**TP-102**

Square red clay teapot with applique design

H：11.5cm　　W：17.5cm

甕形朱泥壺　　競媚清香款　　TP-066

Jug shaped red clay teapot with mark

H：9cm　W：13cm

高梨朱泥壺　　詩句孟臣款　　TP-289

Pear shaped red clay teapot with Mengchen's signature and poetic inscription

H：8cm　W：9.5cm

荷葉貼花朱泥壺　　**TP-308**

Red clay teapot in applique design

H：7cm　　W：13.5cm

圓珠貼花朱泥壺　　**TP-310**

Round shaped red clay teapot in applique design

H：9cm　　W：15cm

君德鑲金朱泥壺　**TP-068**

Gold inlaid red clay teapot

H：9.5cm　W：14.5cm

君德鑲金朱泥壺　龍印款　**TP-183**

Gold inlaid red clay teapot

H：8cm　W：14cm

圓扁鑲金朱泥壺　畊山款　**TP-063**

Gold inlaid compressed red clay teapot

H：7cm　W：12cm

三足圓扁朱泥壺　詩句孟臣款　**TP-323**

Oblate red clay teapot with three legs with Mengchen's signature and poetic inscription

H：7cm　W：12.5cm

鵝蛋形鑲金朱泥壺　TP-062

Gold inlaid egg shaped red clay teapot

H：9cm　W：10.5cm

笠形鑲銀朱泥壺　孟臣款　TP-065

Silver inlaid red clay teapot marked by Mengchen

H：10.5cm　W：17cm

菊瓣鑲銅朱泥壺　　**TP-572**

Bronze inlaid chrysanthemum petal shaped zisha teapot

H：9cm　W：12cm

（左）鑲銀朱泥小品壺　（右）鑲金朱泥小品壺　　**TP-559**

R : Gold inlaid small red clay teapot　L : Silver inlaid small red clay teapot

H：6.5cm　W：11.7cm（左）

鑲金梨形朱泥壺　　**TP-334**

Gold inlaid pear shaped red clay teapot

H：7.5cm　W：12.5cm

鑲金文旦朱泥壺　**TP-320**

Gold inlaid red clay teapot

H：7.5cm　W：12cm

梅段朱泥壺一對　詩句孟臣款　**TP-345**

A pair of red clay teapot with Mengchen's signature
and poetic inscription

H：8.5cm　W：10cm

四方傳爐朱泥壺　詩句孟臣款　**TP-335**

Square shaped red clay teapot with Mengchen's signature and poetic inscription

H：6.5cm　W：9.5cm

鼓腹朱泥壺　**TP-393**

Compressed red clay teapot

H：7.5cm　W：12cm

芭樂朱泥壺　詩句孟臣款　**TP-064**

Papaya shaped red clay teapot with Mengchen's signature and poetic inscribtion

H：6cm　W：9cm

朱泥小品壺　**TP-570**

A pair of small red clay teapot

H：3.8cm　W：5.5cm

君德朱泥壺　君德款　**TP-161**

Red clay teapot with mark

H：6cm　W：12.5cm

君德朱泥壺　詩句孟臣制款　**TP-145**

Red clay teapot with Mengchen's signature and poetic inscription

H：5cm　W：10cm

束身朱泥壺　　**TP-322**

Red clay teapot

H：6cm　　W：11.5cm

朱泥小品壺　　栢亭款　**TP-592**

Small red clay teapot with mark

H：7.5cm　　W：10cm

四方紅砂壺　　**TP-584**

Square shaped red clay teapot

H：5.5cm　W：12cm

鐘形四方紅砂壺　　　**TP-585**

Square bell shaped red clay teapot

H：6cm　W：7.8cm

古蓮子紫砂壺　　匋齋款　　**TP-195**

Zisha teapot with mark

H：10cm　W：16.5cm

古蓮子紫砂壺　宣統元年月正元日款　**TP-211**

Zisha teapot marked Xuantong period Qing Dynasty

H：10cm　W：16cm

標準形黃泥壺　孟臣款　**TP-055**

Yellow clay teapot marked by Mengchen

H：7.5cm　W：13cm

扁燈拋光紫砂茶壺　高陽貢局款

Compressed and polished zisha teapot

H：7.5cm　W：13.5cm

TP-478

稜角堆泥朱泥壺 **TP-337**

Red clay teapot with slip painted decoration

H：8cm　W：11.5cm

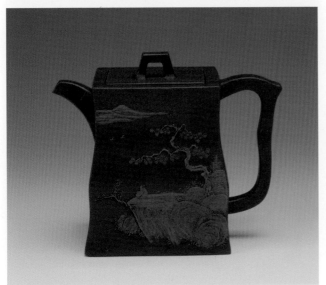

堆泥四方朱泥壺 **TP-208**

Square shaped red clay teapot with stamped pattern

H：9cm　W：11cm

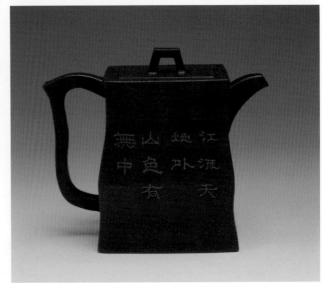

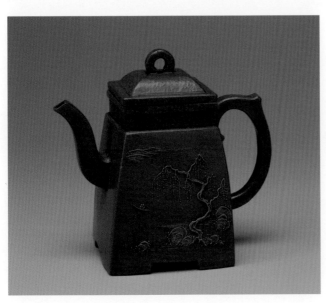

四方鐘形堆泥朱泥壺 **TP-321**

Square bell shaped red clay teapot with slip
painted decoration

H：9.5cm　W：10.5cm

堆泥平蓋朱泥壺　**TP-188**

Red clay teapot with stamped pattern

H：7.5cm　W：11cm

 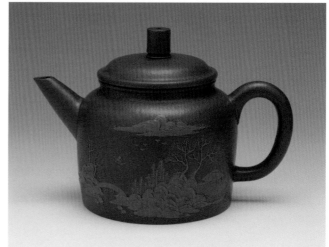

堆泥直筒朱泥壺　**TP-151**

Cylindrical red clay teapot

H：8cm　W：17cm

甕形提樑朱泥壺　　**TP-338**
詩句孟臣款
Jug shaped red clay teapot
with Mengchen's signature
and poetic inscription
H：14.5cm　W：11.5cm

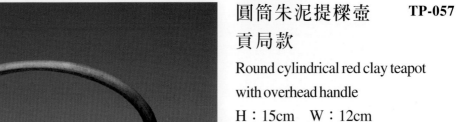

圓筒朱泥提樑壺　　**TP-057**
貢局款
Round cylindrical red clay teapot
with overhead handle
H：15cm　W：12cm

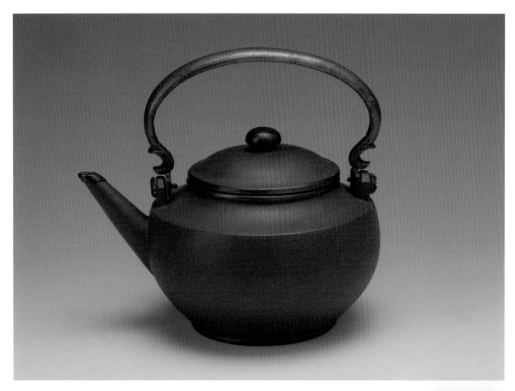

斜角碗形提樑朱泥壺　詩句孟臣款　**TP-243**

Red clay teapot with overhead handle

with Mengchen's signature and poetic inscription

H：12.5cm　W：13.5cm

標準式提樑朱泥壺　**TP-285**

Red clay teapot with overhead handle

H：23.5cm　W：25cm

甕形提樑朱泥壺　TP-287

Jug shaped red clay teapot with overhead handle

H：10.5cm　W：9cm

斜角碗形提樑朱泥壺　TP-339

Bowl shaped red clay teapot with overhead handle

H：15.5cm　W：17cm

扁燈提樑朱泥壺 **TP-146**

Compressed shape red clay teapot with overhead handle

H：10cm　W：11cm

扁燈提樑朱泥壺 **畊山監製** **TP-242**

Compressed shape red clay teapot with overhead handle with mark

H：14cm　W：16cm

扁燈提樑散頭壺　　蕚圊督製款　　**TP-288**

Compressed red clay teapot with overhead handle with mark

H：7.5cm　W：9cm

散頭提樑壺　　**TP-230**

Red clay teapot with overhead handle

H：11cm　W：10.5cm

紫砂直流壺　**TP-126**

Cylindrical zisha teapots

H：7.5cm　W：11.5cm

平蓋紫砂小品壺一對　萬豐順記款　**JTP-492**

A pair of zisha teapot with mark

H：9.5cm　W：5cm

平蓋紫砂小品壺一對　萬豐順記款　**JTP-488**

A pair of zisha teapots with mark

H：10cm　W：5cm

甕形紫砂壺一對　**JTP-489**

A pair of jug shaped zisha teapots

H：7.5cm　W：10.5cm

菊瓣梨皮紫砂小品壺一對　**JTP-490**

A pair of chrysanthemum petal shape zisha teapots

H：5cm　W：8cm

梨形紫砂小品一對　森峰雅樂款　**JTP-793**

A pair of pearl shaped zisha teapots

H：6cm　W：10cm

菊瓣梨皮紫砂小品壺一對　**JTP-491**

A pair of chrysanthemum petal shape zisha teapots

H：5cm　W：8.5cm

甕形朱泥壺一對　東蒼金石制記款　**JTP-495**

A pair of jug shaped red clay teapots with mark

H：9.5cm　W：13.5cm

甕形紫砂壺一對　**JTP-480**

A pair of jug shaped zisha teapot

H：7.5cm　W：9.5cm

笠蓋墨泥壺　　**JTP-487**

A black clay teapot

H：7.5cm　W：11cm

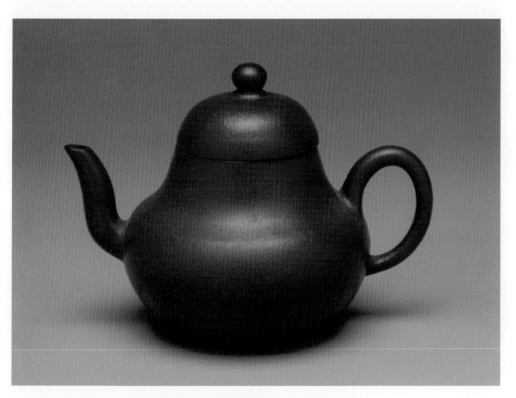

思亭朱泥壺　　龍溪魏梓敬珍藏款　**JTP-485**

Red clay teapot with mark

H：7cm　W：9.5cm

圓扁紫砂小品壺　**JTP-486**

Compressed shape zisha teapot

H：5.5cm　W：11cm

梨形紅砂小品壺　詩句孟臣款　　**JTP-493**

A pair of pearl shaped red clay teapots with Mengchen's signature and poetic inscription

H：7.5cm　W：11.5cm

直桶腰線紫砂壺一對　萬寶款　　　**JTP-482**

A pair of zisha teapots with waist line design with mark

H：6.5cm　　W：9.5cm

紫砂小品壺一對　**JTP-481**

A pair of zisha teapots

H：6.5cm　　W：9.5cm

標準形紫砂壺一對　**JTP-483**

A pair of zisha teapots

H：6.5cm　W：12.5cm

心經墨泥壺一對　**JTP-494**

A pair of black clay teapots inscribed with Chinese " Xi Gen "

H：6.5cm　W：10cm

滲砂紫砂小壺一對 TP-571

A pair of Zisha teapots

H：6.5cm　W：9cm

滲砂紫砂小品壺 TP-545

Zisha teapots with waist line design

H：7cm　W：8.5cm（左）

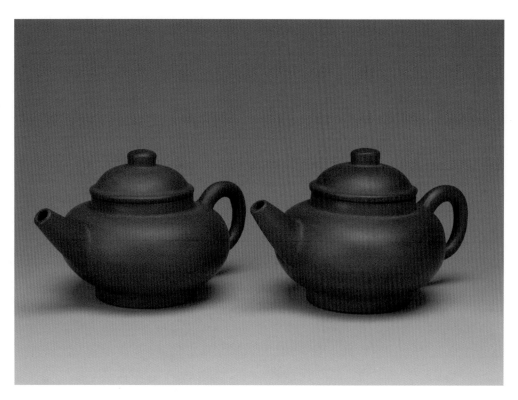

紫砂小品壺一對　**TP-583**

A pair of Zisha teapots

H：6.5cm　W：11cm

朱泥小品壺　**TP-548**

Small red clay teapots

H：7cm　W：9.5cm（左）

甕形朱砂壺　**TP-159**

Jug shaped red clay teapot

H：9cm　W：13cm

平蓋直筒紫砂壺　**TP-392**

Cylindrical zisha teapot with flat lid

H：10.5cm　W：15cm

（左）青灰砂小品壺　（右）紫砂小品壺　**TP-551**

L : Small green clay teapot　R : Small zisha teapot

H：4.5cm　W：10cm（左）

紫砂小品壺　**TP-550**

Small zisha teapots

H：6cm　W：11cm（左）

紫砂小品壺　**TP-549**

Small zisha teapots

H：6.5cm　W：10.8cm（左）

紅砂小品壺一對　**TP-582**

A pair of red clay teapots

H：8.5cm　W：11cm（左）

朱泥小品壺　**TP-555**

Small red clay teapots

H：5cm　W：9cm（左）

朱泥小品壺　**TP-554**

Small red clay teapots

H：7cm　W：10cm（左）

紫砂小品壺三把　　**TP-547**

Three small zisha teapots

H：8cm　　W：9.7cm（左）

紫砂滲砂小品壺三把　　**TP-546**

Three small zisha teapots

H：6.5cm　　W：9.5cm（左）

朱泥水平小品壺　**TP-556**

Small red clay teapots

H：3.5cm　W：6cm（左）

藍釉紫砂小品壺　**TP-561**

Small zisha teapots in blue glaze

H：6cm　W：10cm（左）

獅鈕紅泥小品　**TP-558**

Small red clay teapots with lion knob

H：4.5cm　W：7.7cm（左）

獅鈕紅泥小品壺　　**TP-557**

Small red clay teapots with lion knob

H：4.5cm　W：8.2cm（左）

紫砂小品壺　**TP-552**

Small zisha teapots

H：6.5cm　W：10.7cm（左）

紫砂小品壺　**TP-553**

Small zisha teapots

H：6.5cm　W：10.7cm（左）

均釉紫砂壺　**TP-591**

Zisha teapot in blue jun glaze

H：8cm　W：14cm

藍釉圓扁紫砂壺　**TP-535**

Oblate shaped zisha teapot in blue glaze

H：9.5cm　W：16cm

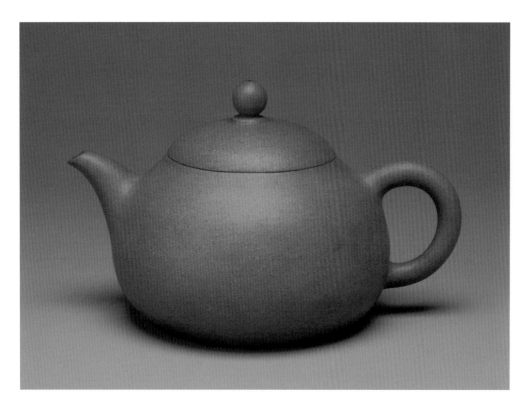

西施段泥壺　TP-538

Blended clay teapot

H：9.5cm　W：14.5cm

心經黃泥壺　鐵畫軒製　TP-139

Yellow clay teapot inscribed of Chinese calligraphy "xin Gen"

H：7cm　W：11cm

柏樂朱泥壺　陽羨惜陰室王款　**JTP-484**

A pair of clay teapot with mark

H：6.5cm　W：10.5cm

圓扁紫砂壺　張君德制　**TP-389**

Oblate shaped zisha teapot with mark

H：7.5cm　W：15cm

朱泥滿天星茶壺　**TP-653**

Red clay teapot

H：10cm　W：13.3cm

龍旦朱泥壺　**TP-180**

Egg shaped red clay teapot

H：10.5cm　W：13.5cm

堆泥壽紋紫砂壺　　TP-326

Zisha teapot in applique design

H：10.5cm　W：16cm

碗形如意扭紫砂壺　　TP-324

Bowl shaped zisha teapot with Ruyi knob

H：12cm　W：17.5cm

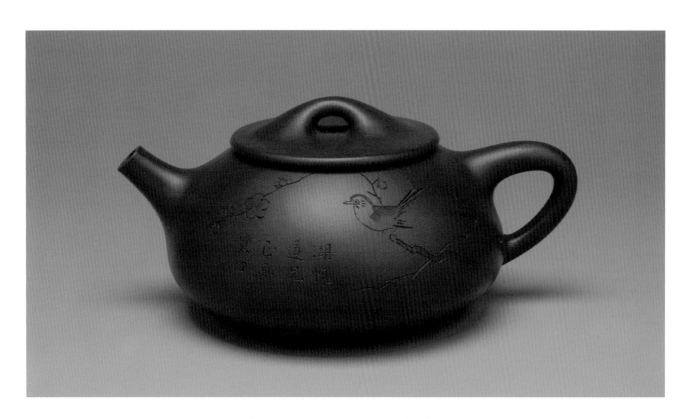

石瓢紫砂壺　景舟制款　　　**TP-325**

Stone weight shaped zisha teapot with mark

H：7.5cm　W：16.5cm

石瓢紫砂壺　武陵逸人款　**TP-141**

Stone weight shaped zisha teapot with mark

H：7.5cm　W：17.5cm

扁腹紫砂壺　顧景洲款　**TP-162**

Compressed zisha teapot with mark

H：8cm　W：16cm

蓮藕黃泥酒器　**TP-344**
蔣蓉款

Lotus roots shaped yellow
clay wine vessel with mark

H：22cm　W：18cm

竹節日蒸紫砂壺　汪寅仙款　　**TP-099**

Zisha teapot in bamboo section shape with mark

H：18cm　W：13cm

蟠螭供春紫砂壺　寅仙款　　**TP-112**

Zisha teapot with carved hornless dragon design with mark

H：10.8cm　　W：18.5cm

扁腹彩泥紫砂壺　汪寅仙制款　**TP-315**

Compressed and painted zisha teapot with mark

H：6.5cm　W：14.5cm

佛手椿紫砂壺　汪寅仙款　　**TP-381**

Zisha teapot in the shape of Buddha's hand citron with mark

H：12.5cm　W：16.5cm

圓扁竹段紫砂壺　　何道洪制款　　**TP-222**

Oblate shaped zisha teapot with bamboo section design with mark

H：9cm　　W：17cm

TP-245

道方紫砂壺　道洪製匋款
Square shaped zisha teapot
with mark
H：17cm　W：16cm

博浪鎚紫砂壺　劉海粟書鮑仲梅款　**TP-088**

Zisha teapot with a chian shot design with signature's
of Bao Zhong Mei and Liu Hai Shu

H：10.5cm　W：12cm

方鐘形紫砂壺　潘持平製　**TP-091**

Square bell shaped zisha teapot

H：12cm　W：17cm

亞明四方紫砂壺　潘持平款　**TP-103**

Square shaped zisha teapot with mark

H：11cm　W：18.5cm

三足鳳流黃泥壺　　遞華款　　　**TP-542**

Yellow clay teapot with three legs design with mark

H：9cm　W：9.5cm

玉泉紫砂壺　　錦鋒公司贈款　TP-586

Zisha teapot with mark

H：6.5cm　W：11.5cm

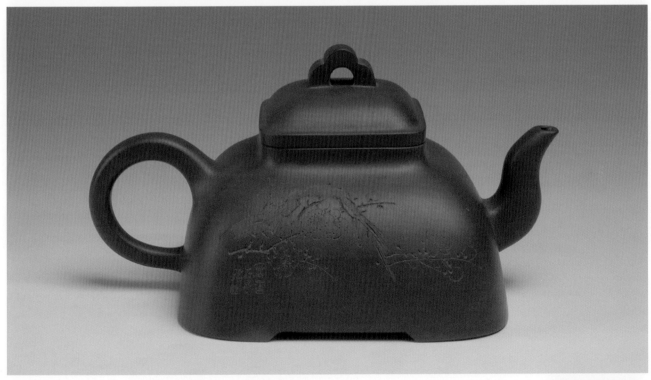

瓟稜紫砂壺　葛明仙款　**TP-104**

Melon shaped zisha teapot with Gemingxian's signature

H：9.5cm　W：17.5cm

葫瓜形蟋蟀綠泥壺　壺癮王度款　　**TP-588**

Calabash shaped green glaze teapot with mark of Mr. Tu Wang

H：9.8cm　W：14cm

高風亮節綠泥壺　顧紹培製　**TP-304**

Green glaze teapot in bamboo section design with mark

H：23cm　W：20cm

漢方紫砂提樑壺　周桂珍造款　**TP-358**

Zisha teapot with overhead handle of the Han style and the signature of Zhou Gui Zhen

H：15.5cm　W：14cm

印袍紫砂壺　周桂珍造款　**TP-155**

Zisha teapot with the signature of Zhou Gui Zhen

H：9.5cm　W：16.5cm

圓珠紫砂壺　李碧芳製款　**TP-219**

Round shaped zisha teapot with mark

H：10cm　W：16cm

城鈕圓扁紫砂壺　呂堯臣製款　　**TP-328**

Oblate shaped zisha teapot with mark

H：10cm　W：17.5cm

綾花紫砂壺　堯臣壺款 **TP-154**

Zisha teapot with mark

H：11cm　W：16cm

四方城牆紫砂壺　　紹培制匋款　　**TP-218**
Square shaped zisha teapot with mark
H：11.5cm　　W：18cm

四方城牆提樑紫砂壺　　紹培制匋款　　**TP-327**
Square shaped zisha teapot of overhead handle with mark
H：17cm　　W：14.5cm

上心橋紫砂壺　沈漢生制　**TP-359**

Zisha teapot of arch shape knob with mark

H：9cm　W：18.5cm

圈線四方紫砂壺　昌鴻款　**TP-380**

Square shaped zisha teapot with mark

H：14cm　W：19cm

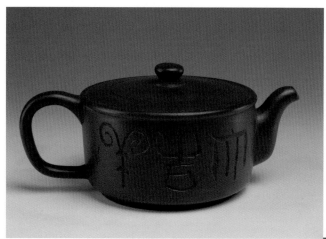

圓盾紫砂壺　**TP-119**

Targe shaped zisha teapot with mark

H：7.3cm　W：17.5cm

樹癭供春黃泥壺　四海陶製款　**TP-086**

Tree knur shaped yellow clay teapot with mark

H：11cm　W：17cm

水仙花紫砂壺　葛陶中製款　　**TP-106**

Zisha teapot of narcissus design with mark

H：8cm　W：17cm

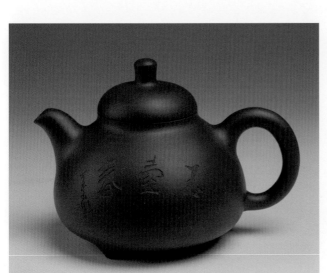

乳鼎紫砂壺　高振宇製款　**TP-117**

Zisha teapot with mark

H：10m　W：15cm

袖珍型各式紫砂小品壺　高建芳創作　**TP-569**

A group of small zisha teapots

H：3.6cm　W：4.6cm（左上）

綠泥西瓜壺　高建芳款　**TP-122**

Watermelon shaped green clay teapot with mark

H：10cm　W：17cm

圓珠紫砂壺　陳國良製款　**TP-360**

Round shaped zisha teapot with mark

H：10.5cm　W：16.5cm

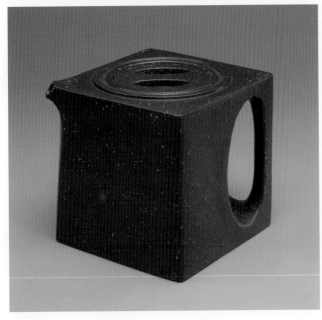

滲砂大方壺紫砂　吳群祥制款　**TP-121**

Large square zisha teapot with mark

H：9.5cm　W：10cm

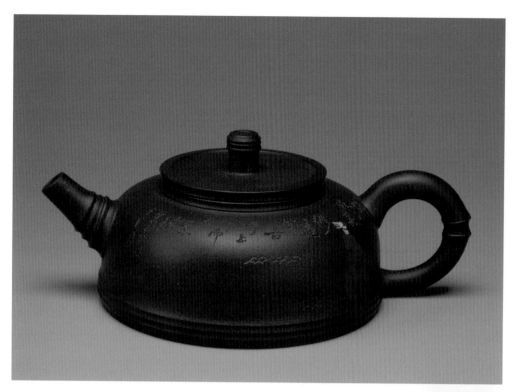

半圓竹節紫砂壺　集泉壺款　　　　　**TP-312**

Green stripe zisha teapot of bamboon section design with mark

H：6.5cm　W：16cm

六方竹節紫砂壺　集泉壺款　**TP-160**

Hexagonal zisha teapot with bamboo section design with mark

H：5.5cm　W：14cm

六方提樑紫砂壺　　定華款　**TP-172**

Hexagonal zisha teapot of overhead handle
with mark
H：14cm　W：15.5cm

兩截式四方紫砂茶具套組　　**TP-366**

A set of square Zisha teapot and cups
H：13cm　W：15cm

絞泥合歡紫砂壺　　**TP-305**

Twisted clay zisha teapot

H：8cm　W：16.5cm

圓扁波浪紫砂壺　徐娟制款　**TP-309**

Oblate shaped zisha teapot with mark

H：8cm　W：15.5cm

鳳流龍把黃泥壺　**TP-382**

Yellow clay teapot with phoenix design lid and dragon shape knob

H：13.5cm　W：17cm

龍鈕縷空紫砂壺　**TP-271**

Ziasha teapot in openwork with dragon knob

H：11.5cm　W：19.5cm

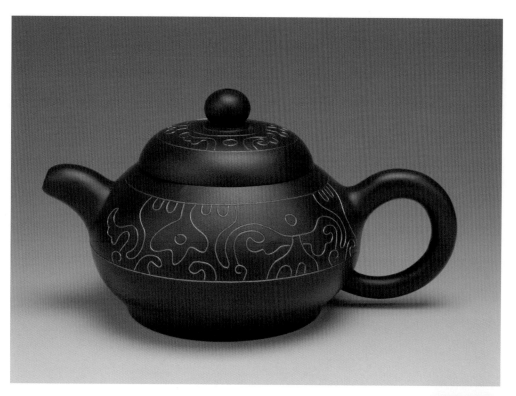

鑲金紫砂壺　何燕萍製款　**TP-205**

Gold inlaid zisha teapot with mark

H：8.5cm　W：17cm

笠蓋輟球紫砂壺　何燕萍制款　　**TP-163**

Globular zisha teapot of lid with mark

H：13.5cm　W：18cm

三足砲管提樑紫砂壺　**TP-332**

Zisha teapot with overhead handle and three legged

H：14cm　W：21cm

巧形刻字紫砂壺一對　**TP-544**

A pair of zisha teapots

H：14.5cm　W：13.5cm（左）

錢幣扁燈紫砂壺　　**TP-272**

Compressed zisha teapot with coin design knob

H：11cm　　W：25.5cm

瓜形朱泥壺　　　**TP-365**

Melon shaped red clay teapot

H：11.5cm　　W：22cm

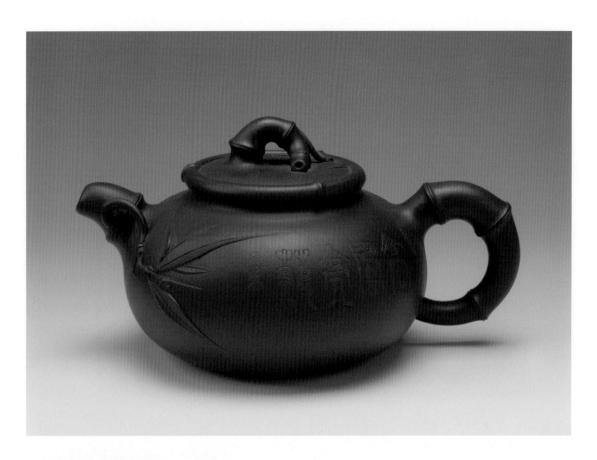

竹節圓扁紫砂壺　**TP-156**

Oblate shaped zisha teapot with bamboo section design

H：9cm　W：18cm

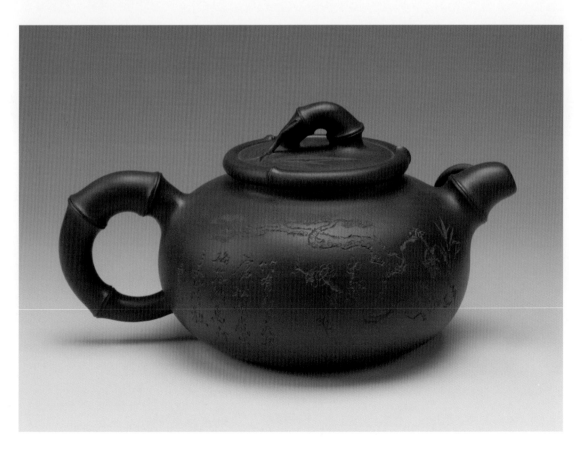

梅椿紫砂壺　**TP-565**

Plum tree trunk shaped zisha teapot

H：10cm　W：14cm

三足松竹梅紫泥壺　　周榮金製款　**TP-504**

L : Zisha teapot with three legged　R: Yellow glaze teapot

H：9cm　W：15.5cm（左）

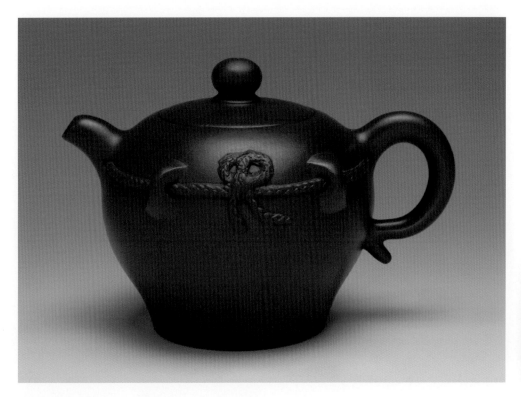

腰帶紫砂壺　群祥款　**TP-398**

Zisha teapot with mark

H：10cm　W：14cm

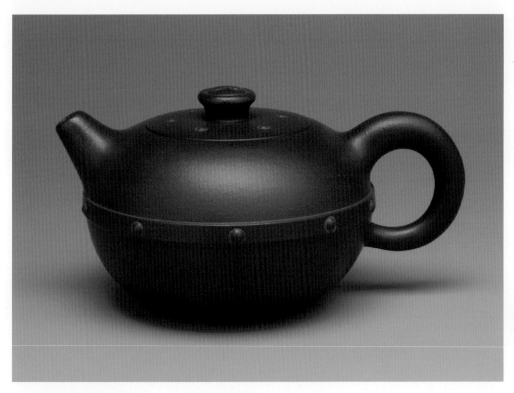

圓珠腰線紫砂壺　許美華製款　**TP-361**

Round shaped zisha teapot

H：7.5cm　W：15cm

獅鈕四方斜身紫砂壺　**TP-526**

Square shaped zisha teapot with lion knob

H：13.5cm　W：14cm

四方紫砂壺　魏橋花制款　**TP-094**

Square shaped zisha teapot with mark

H：19.5cm　W：15.5cm

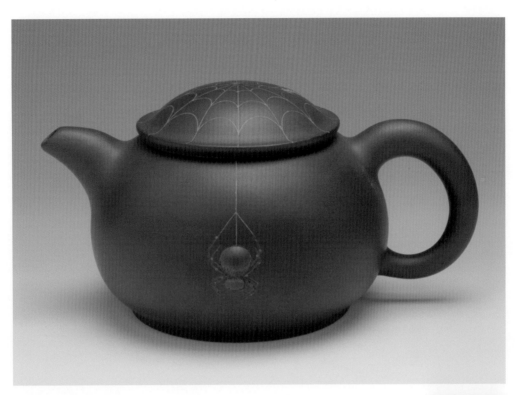

蜘蛛網綠泥壺　　**TP-182**

Green glazed teapot

H：7.5cm　W：15cm

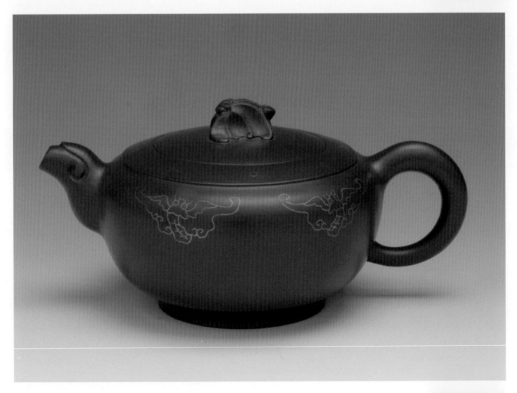

嵌銀圓扁紫砂壺　　**TP-210**

Silver inlaid oblate zisha teapot

H：6.5cm　W：14.5cm

三足套杯紫砂茶具組　尹紅娣款　**TP-387**

A set of zisah teapot and three legged cups with mark

H：11.5cm　W：16cm（茶壺）

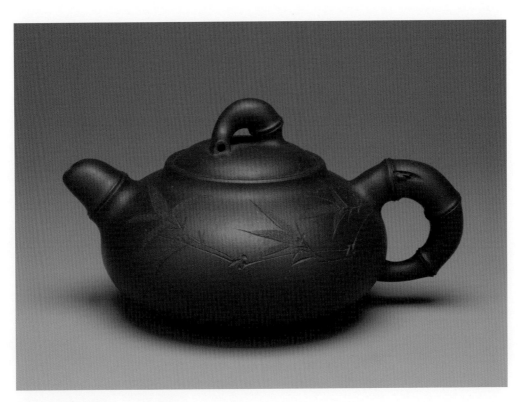

矮竹紫砂壺　TP-566

Zisha teapot with bamboo section design

H：8cm　W：15cm

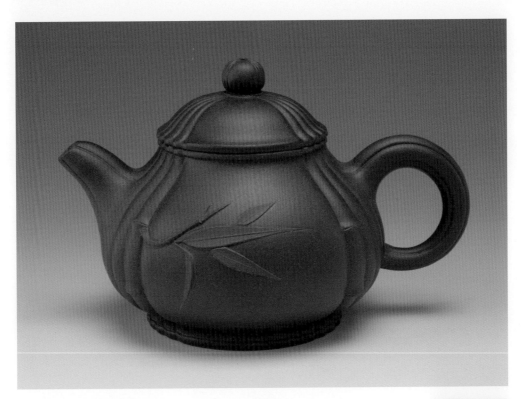

高潘式竹節紫砂壺　陳氏壺藝款　TP-186

Zisha teapot of bamboo section design with mark

H：9.5cm　W：15cm

圓扁竹節朱泥壺　鮑燕萍制款　　**TP-329**

Oblate shaped red clay teapot of bamboo section design with mark

H：7cm　W：16.5cm

松竹梅菱形紫砂壺　**TP-533**

Diamond shaped zisha teapot with pine, bamboo and plum design

H：10cm　W：14.5cm

圓扁紫砂壺 **TP-166**

Oblate shaped zisha teapot

H：6.5cm　W：15cm

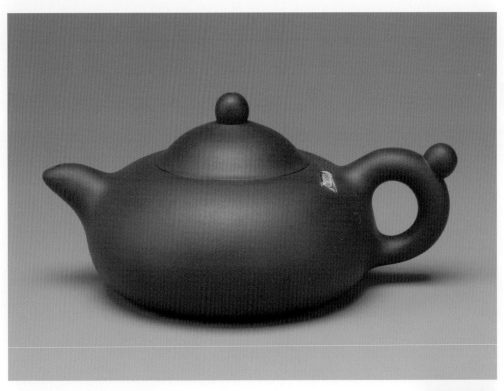

圓扁紫砂壺 **TP-319**

Oblate shaped zisha teapot with mark

H：6.5cm　W：14cm

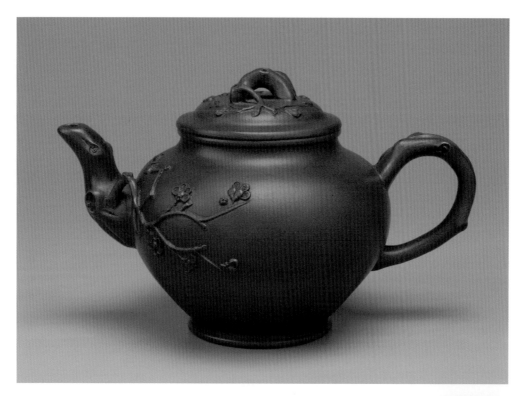

梅花報春紫砂壺　中國宜興款　　**TP-165**

Zisha teapot with plum design

H：19cm　W：11.5cm

松竹梅三報春紫砂壺　中國宜興款　　**TP-388**

Zisha teapots with pine, bamboo and plum design

H：8.5cm　W：13cm(左1)

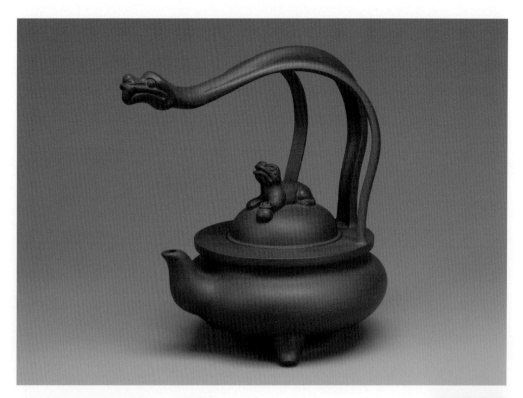

三足龍把紫砂壺　**TP-362**

Zisha teapot with three legs and dragon shape handle

H：16.5cm　W：15.5cm

三足羊鈕紫砂壺　**TP-384**

Zisha teapot with three legs and lamb shape knob

H：12cm　W：17cm

刻花甕形紫砂壺　**TP-209**

Jug shaped red clay teapot carved with flower pattern

H：10cm　W：14cm

鏤空巧雕龍把墨泥壺　**TP-564**

Black clay teapot with carved dragon design in open work

H：10.5cm　W：18cm

四方斜角滲砂紫砂壺　**TP-531**

Square zisha teapot

H：7cm　W：14.5cm

僧帽紫砂壺　蔣德寅製款　**TP-090**

Monk cap shaped zisha teapot with mark

H：17.5cm　W：13.5cm

圓扁刻畫黃泥壺　王紅娟制款　**TP-383**

Oblate shaped yellow clay teapot carved of painting with mark

H：10cm　W：16cm

圓扁肩線綠泥壺　曉軍制陶款　**TP-385**

Oblate shaped green glaze teapot with mark

H：7cm　W：13cm

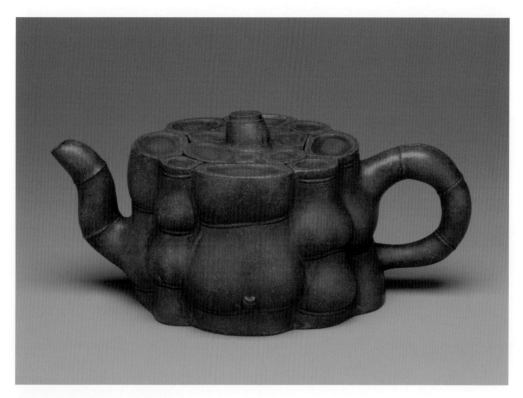

捆竹紫砂壺　TP-563

Zisha teapot in the shape of buddled bamboo section

H：8cm　W：17cm

菊半束腰紫砂壺　TP-198

Chrysanthemum petal shaped zisha teapot

H：9.5cm　W：15cm

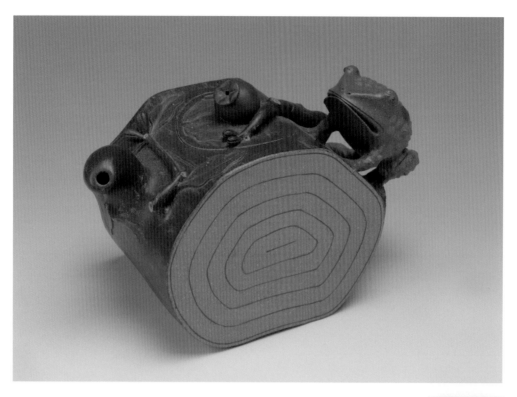

石榴樹蛙黃泥壺　蔣藝華制款　　**TP-223**

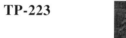

Yellow clay teapot of flog design with mark

H：9cm　W：14cm

獻桃紅泥壺　**TP-528**

Peach shaped red clay teapot

H：9.5cm　W：15cm

佛手黃泥壺　TP-525

Yellow clay teapot in the shape of Buddha's hand citron

H：10cm　W：17cm

獻桃紫砂壺　TP-527

Peach shaped zisha teapot

H：10.5cm　W：19cm

樹癭供春壺　TP-524

Tree knur shaped teapot

H：9cm　W：15cm

鐘形紫砂壺　TP-177

Bell shaped zisha teapot

H：14cm　W：8.5cm

菊瓣肩線朱泥壺　李園林制款　　**TP-378**
Cylindrical chrysanthemum petal shaped red clay teapot with mark
L14cm　H11cm

四方包袱紫砂壺　**TP-330**
Square zisha teapot in wrapped cloth shape
H：10.5cm　W：18.5cm

肖像扁腹紫砂壺　毅群陶業款　**TP-534**

Compressed zisha teapot

H：7.5cm　W：13cm

印花綴球朱泥壺　　**TP-157**

Globular red clay teapot in applique design

H：10cm　W：14.5cm

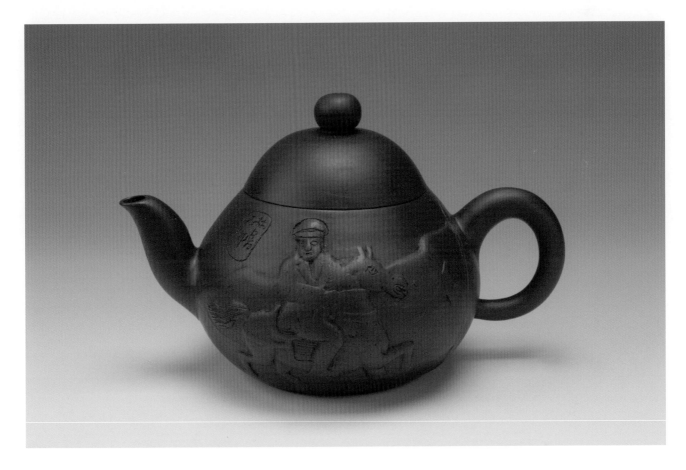

印花梨形朱泥壺　　**TP-158**

Pear shaped red clay teapot in applique design

H：10cm　W：16.5cm

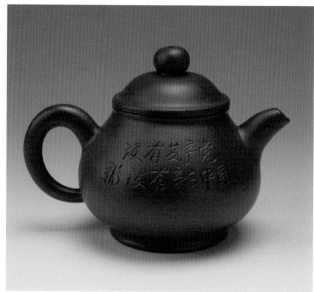

高潘式印花朱泥壺　**TP-176**

Red clay teapot in applique design

H：10cm　W：14cm

石瓢印花朱泥壺　**TP-170**

Stone weight shaped red clay teapot with stamp prints

H：7cm　W：15cm

蓮子綴球印花朱泥壺　　**TP-173**

Globular red clay teapot

H：10.5cm　　W：15cm

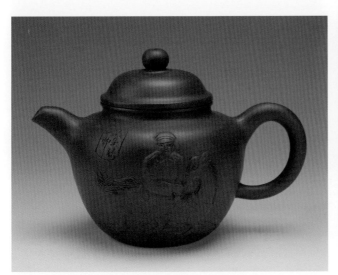 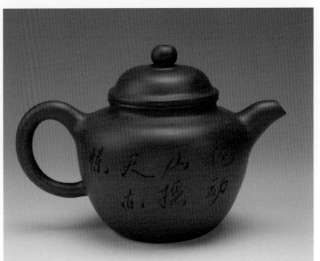

蓮子綴球印花朱泥壺　　**TP-174**

Globular red clay teapot

H：10cm　　W：15cm

 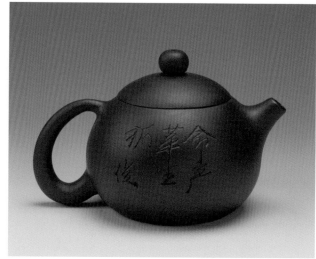

倒把西施印花朱泥壺　　**TP-175**

Red clay teapot with flower patterns

H：8.5cm　W：13.5cm

龍旦印花朱泥壺　　　　**TP-169**

Egg shaped red clay teapot with applique design

H：10.5cm　W：13cm

國父紀念紫砂壺　**TP-226**

Zisha teapot with Dr. San Yet sen's image

H：10cm　W：16.5cm

國父紀念紫砂壺　**TP-225**

Zisha teapot with Dr. San Yet sen's image

H：8.5cm　W：15.5cm

稜花直筒紫砂壺   **TP-190**
清德堂
Cylindrical zisha teapot
H：16cm　W：13.5cm

刻字山水紫砂壺   **TP-191**
Zisha teapot with landscape design
H：12.5cm　W：13.5cm

稜角半月紫砂壺   **TP-307**
Half moon shaped zisha teapot
H：9.5cm　W：15.5cm

紫砂大提樑 TP-700

Zisha teapot with large overhead handle

H：162cm　W：92cm

紫砂東坡大提樑　TP-699

Large zisha teapot in Dougpo style with overhead handle

H：112cm　W：60cm

紫砂大提樑　TP-698

Zisha teapot with large overhead handle

H：64cm　W：67cm

上釉雕花提樑壺　**TP-275**

Lacquer carved teapot with overhead handle

H：48cm　W：37cm

上釉高風亮節壺　**TP-276**

Glazed teapot with bamboo section design

H：51cm　　W：51cm

上釉雕花竹節壺　**TP-274**

Lacquer carved bamboo design teapot

H：51cm　　W：56cm

南瓜黃泥提樑壺 　 **TP-148**
王南君制款

Pumpkin shaped yellow clay teapot
of overhead handle with mark

H：14cm　　W：15.5cm

東坡提樑紫砂壺 　 **TP-293**

Zisha teapot in Dougpo style with
overhead handle

H：34cm　　W：26cm

鐘形錫包紫砂壺　TP-032

Bell shaped pewter encesed zisha teapot

H：12cm　W：15.5cm

　　以錫作器，自古有之。宋人曾有「茶宜錫」的記載。約於清道光年間（西元1821至1850年）太湖之濱興起一種新工藝－包錫紫砂茶壺，意即在紫砂壺外包錫皮，使之相結合成型，蓋紐與壺把、壺嘴則用玉石鑲接。錫片上刻畫詩文繪畫，高雅別緻，不失爲一種有特色的裝飾方法。

　　朱石楳、楊彭年、瞿應紹、沈存周等人爲當時著名製壺名家。

笠形錫包紫砂壺　　**TP-031**

Zisha teapot encased with pewter

H：10cm　W：15.5cm

四方鐘形錫包紫砂壺　**TP-019**

Square bell shaped pewter encesed zisha teapot

H：10.5cm　W：13.5cm

四方錫包紫砂壺　**TP-024**

Square pewter encased zisha teapot

H：10cm　W：14.5cm

四方錫包紫砂壺　**TP-027**

Square pewter encased zisha teapot

H：10.5cm　W：15cm

六方斜角錫包紫砂壺　**TP-021**

Hexagonal pewter encased zisha teapot

H：7.5cm　W：15cm

六方斜角錫包紫砂壺　**TP-023**

Hexagonal pewter encased zisha teapot

H：8cm　W：17cm

四方切角錫包紫砂壺　**TP-046**

Square pewter teapot encased with zisha

H：9cm　W：16cm

六方菱形錫包紫砂壺　**TP-026**

Hexagonal diamond shaped pewter teapot encased with zisha

H：9cm　W：17.5cm

四方磚形錫包紫砂壺　**TP-048**

Square brick shaped pewter teapot encased with zisha

H：9.5cm　W：15.5cm

四方磚形錫包紫砂壺　**TP-020**

Square brick shaped pewter teapot encased zisha

H：8.3cm　W：15.5cm

月形錫包紫砂壺　**TP-049**

Moon shaped pewter teapot encased with zisha

H：9.5cm　W：15cm

花朵形錫包紫砂壺　**TP-037**

Flower shaped pewter teapot encased with zisha

H：9cm　W：17.5cm

四方斜角錫包紫砂壺　TP-028

Square pewter teapot encased with zisha

H：7cm　W：14.5cm

四方磚形錫包紫砂壺　TP-047

Square brick shaped pewter teapot encased with zisha

H：8.8cm　W：16.7cm

六方斜角錫包紫砂壺　**TP-035**

Hexagonal pewter teapot encased with zisha

H：6.5cm　W：16cm

六方開光錫包紫砂壺　**TP-022**

Hexagonal pewter teapot encased with zisha

H：9.5cm　W：16cm

五方切角錫包紫砂壺　**TP-033**

Pentagonal pewter teapot encasted with zisha

H：10cm　W：15cm

235

圓形錫包紫砂壺　**TP-025**

Round pewter teapot encased with zisha

H：7cm　W：16cm

包袱形錫包紫砂壺　**TP-029**

Pewter teapot encased with zisha in the shape of a wrapped cloth

H：7.5cm　W：14cm

圓扁錫包紫砂壺　TP-018

Compressed pewter teapot encased with zisha

H：7cm　W：16.5cm

四方斜角錫包紫砂壺　TP-052

Square pewter teapot encased with zisha

H：9cm　W：14.5cm

圓竹錫包紫砂壺　　**TP-036**

Round pewter teapot encased with zisha

H：8.5cm　W：14.5cm

圓竹節錫包紫砂壺　　**TP-034**

Round teapot encased with zisha in bamboo section shape

H：9cm　W：16.5cm

井欄形錫包紫砂壺　**TP-050**

Pewter teapot emcased with zisha

H：9cm　W：16cm

鐘形錫包紫砂壺　　**TP-051**

Bell shaped pewter teapot encased with zisha

H：9cm　W：14.5cm

TP-479

朱泥壺保溫茶套組

A set of red clay tea
bowl warmer

H：3.5cm　W：5.5cm

　　紫砂茶具起始於宋，盛於明清，流傳至今。在明代中葉以後，逐漸形成了集造型、詩詞、書法、繪畫、篆刻、雕塑於一體的紫砂藝術。紫砂壺原以其自身的造型變化和泥料色澤爲裝飾手段，到清代初期則出現了加釉施彩等多種裝飾工藝，這是與紫砂壺作爲貢品進入宮廷，而皇室崇尚絢麗華貴的風氣相關。

　　康熙皇帝博學多才，喜歡西洋傳入之琺瑯彩，此時期多有金胎、銀胎、玻璃胎、瓷胎和宜興紫砂胎等各種不同質地的琺瑯製品，金碧輝煌。到了乾隆皇帝，其喜好的富麗堂皇的裝飾風格，把餿金、描金、模印、刻劃、雕刻、彩泥堆繪等技法運用在紫砂壺，紫砂胎彩漆描金壺堪稱一絕。

　　紫砂壺裝飾工藝還有拋光、鑲金邊、包錫、包銅等技法，借鑒於金銀工藝技法，先在紫砂壺坯體上刻飾好細緻的紋樣，紋樣的線條均爲陰文，經燒成後再嵌入金、銀、銅等金屬絲，然後整平磨光，用作鑲嵌的金屬材料，由於黃金太昂貴，一般人多以銅及銀絲來代替。其中拋光是將紫砂壺通體打磨光滑，經過拋光處理的紫砂壺，表面光鑒照人，主要出口泰國。鑲金邊是在壺的口沿，嘴的流口，底的邊緣，蓋的周邊及紐等部位，以黃金薄片包鑲，富麗輝煌。包銅、銀邊的紫砂茶壺通常在宜興訂燒，然後運到山東威海衛加工包銅，清末光緒時製作多，主要出口泰國等東南亞地區。

標準形提樑紫砂大壺　**TP-294**

Large zisha teapot with overhead handle

H：28.5cm　W：32cm

243

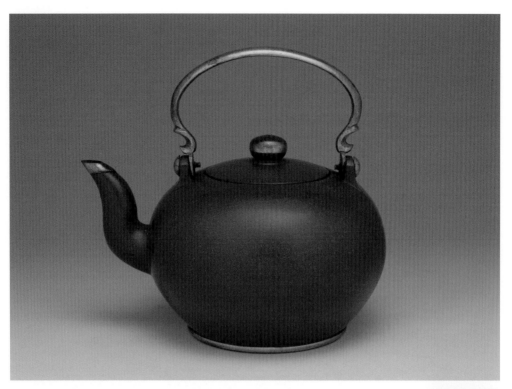

圓珠提樑紫砂壺　　動物印款　**TP-474**

Round shaped zisha teapot of bronze overhead handle with mark

H：17.5cm　　W：19cm

扁腹提樑紫砂壺　　蔣禎祥造款　**TP-284**

Compressed zisha teapot of overhead handle with mark

H：18.5cm　　W：18cm

扁腹提樑紫砂壺　**TP-279**

Compressed zisha teapot with overhead handle

H：17cm　W：20cm

圓珠提樑紫砂壺　龍印款　**TP-040**

Round shaped zisha teapot of overhead handle with mark

H：18cm　W：19.5cm

直筒提樑紫砂壺　　**TP-282**

Cylindrical Zisha teapot with overhead handle

H：20.5cm　W：14.5cm

圓珠提樑紫砂壺　**TP-060**

Round shaped zisha teapot with overhead handle

H：18cm　W：19.5cm

圓珠提樑紫砂壺　　**TP-280**

Round shaped zisha teapot with overhead handle

H：20.5cm　W：21.5cm

圓珠提樑紫砂壺　　**TP-038**

Round shaped zisha teapot with overhead handle

H：15.5cm　W：17cm

直筒提樑紫砂壺　　TP-124

Cylindrical Zisha teapot
with overhead handle
H：20.5cm　W：

直筒提樑紫砂壺　　　TP-473

Cylindrical zisha teapot
with bronze overhead handle
H：20cm　W：15.6cm

圓珠提樑紫砂壺　**TP-059**

Round shaped zisha teapot with overhead handle

H：16cm　W：18cm

圓珠提樑紫砂壺　**TP-045**

Round shaped zisha teapot with overhead handle

H：16cm　W：17.5cm

甕形提樑紫砂壺　詩句孟臣款

Jug shaped zisha teapot with overhead
handle and Mengchen's signature and
poetic inscription

H：18.5cm　W：16.5cm　　**TP-281**

圓珠提樑紫砂壺　**TP-041**

Round shaped zisha teapot with overhead handle

H：16.5cm　W：18cm

圓珠黃泥提樑壺　貢局款**TP-042**

Round yellow clay teapot with overhead handle

H：16cm　W：18cm

圓珠黃泥提樑壺　貢局款　　**TP-283**

Yellow clay teapot with overhead handle

H：18cm　W：20cm

圓珠提樑紫砂壺　**TP-044**

Round shaped zisha teapot with overhead handle

H：20cm　W：23cm

圓珠提樑紫砂壺　**TP-241**

Standard zisha teapot with overhead handle

H：18cm　W：19.5cm（右）

直筒提樑紫砂壺　**TP-123**

Cylindrical Zisha teapot
with overhead handle

H：19.5cm　W：15cm

扁燈提樑紫砂壺　**TP-043**

Compressed zisha teapot with overhead handle

H：19cm　W：24cm

扁燈提樑紫砂壺　詩句孟臣款　**TP-239**

Compressed zisha teapot with overhead handle
and Mengchen's signature and poetic inscription

H：13cm　W：17cm

扁燈提樑墨泥壺　詩句孟臣款　**TP-240**

Compressed black clay teapot with overhead handle
and Mengchen's signature and poetic inscriptione

H：13cm　W：16.5cm

扁燈提樑黃泥壺　　**TP-477**
詩句孟臣款

Oblate shaped yellow clay teapot with bronze
overhead handle and Mengchen's signature and
poetic inscription
H：15.5cm　W：23.5cm

扁燈提樑黃泥壺　　　**TP-476**
高陽款

Oblate shaped yellow clay teapot
of bronze overhead handle with mark
H：13.5cm　W：15.5cm（左）

扁燈提樑黃泥壺　**TP-277**

Compressed yellow clayteapot with overhead
handle
H：17cm　W：22cm

255

扁燈提樑紫砂壺　**TP-056**

Compressed zisha teapot with overhead handle

H：12.5cm　W：10.5cm

TP-475

扁燈提樑紫砂壺　貢局款

Oblate shaped zisha teapot
with bronze overhead handle

H：17cm　W：21cm

扁燈提樑紫砂壺　**TP-039**

Compressed zisha teapot with overhead handle

H：20cm　W：25cm

扁燈提樑紫砂壺　**TP-058**

Compressed zisha teapot with overhead handle

H：13.5cm　W：15cm

扁腹提樑紫砂壺　**TP-286**

Compressed zisha teapot with overhead handle

H：14cm　W：17cm

扁燈提樑紫砂壺　**TP-278**

Compressed zisha teapot with overhead handle

H：15cm　W：19cm

粉彩藍釉紫砂茶葉罐　王南林制款　**TP-457**

Zisha tea canister in blue and famille rose enamel colors with mark

H：17cm　W：16.5cm

六方雲角朱砂茶葉罐　大彬款　**TP-451**
Hexagonal red clay tea canister with mark
H：12cm　W：9.3cm

四方凹角參砂紫砂茶葉罐　陳萬餘制款　**TP-440**

Square zisha tea canister with mark

H：23.5cm　W：17.5cm

六方甕形紫砂茶葉罐　**TP-444**

L : Hexagonal zisha tea canisters

H：18cm　W：14cm（左）

橄欖形紫砂茶葉罐　**TP-448**

Oliver shaped zisha tea canister

H：16cm　W：13cm

甕形紫砂茶葉葉罐　**TP-431**

Jug shaped zisha tea canisters

H：9cm　W：8cm（左）

甕形紫砂茶葉罐　　TP-430

Jug shaped zisha tea canisters

H：11.5cm　　W：10cm（左）

（左）桶形朱泥茶葉罐　（右）四方紫砂茶葉罐　　TP-432

L : Red clay teapot　R : Square zisha tea canister

H：10.5cm　　W：9cm（左）

朱泥茶葉罐　**TP-445**

L : Red clay tea canister　　R : Zisha tea canister

H：11.5cm　　W：12.3cm（左）

（左）橄欖形黃泥茶葉罐　　（右）橄欖形紫砂茶葉罐　**TP-446**

L : Olive shaped yellow clay tea canister　　R : Oliver shaped zisha tea canister

H：15.5cm　　W：13.5cm（左）

六方紫砂茶葉罐　**TP-450**

L : Hexagonal zisha tea canister　R : Zisha tea canister

H：12cm　W：9.8cm

六方印花紫砂茶罐一對　**TP-447**

Hexagonal zisha tea canisters in applique design

H：23.5cm　W：15.5cm

六方印花紫砂茶葉罐　**TP-472**

Hexagonal tea canister in applique design

H：24cm　W：15.5cm

六方印花紫砂茶葉罐　**TP-077**

Hexagonal tea canister

H：23.5cm　W：16cm

甕形紫砂茶葉罐　TP-439

Jug shaped zisha tea canister

H：18cm　W：16cm

甕形紫砂茶罐　TP-471

Zisha tea canister

H：18cm　W：16.5cm

泥繪紫砂茶葉罐　**TP-436**

Zisha tea canister with slip painted decoration

H：14cm　W：15cm

蓋印龍紋紫砂茶葉罐　悟陶園製款　**TP-441**

Zisha tea canister of dragon pattern lid with mark

H：16.5cm　W：17cm

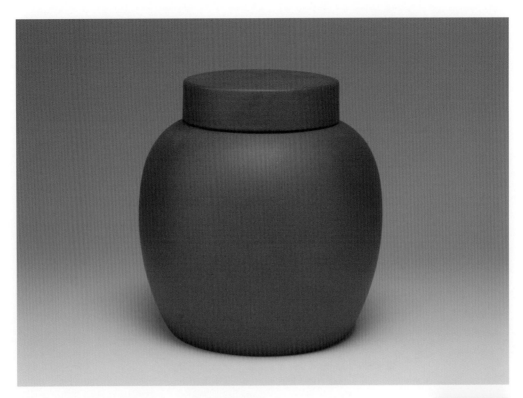

甕形紫砂茶葉罐　悟陶園製款　　**TP-438**

Jug shaped zisha tea canister of flat lid with mark

H：18.5cm　W：17cm

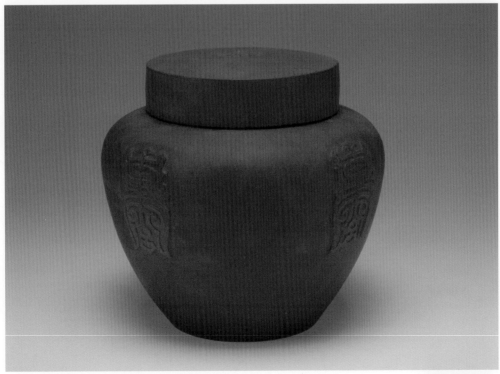

壽紋紫砂茶葉罐　**TP-426**

Zisha tea canister inscribed with Chinese character " longevity"

H：16.5cm　W：17.5cm

竹簑形紫砂茶葉罐　吳益豐制款　**TP-443**

Zisha tea canister with mark

H：8.5cm　W：11cm

竹節式紫砂三層茶葉罐　**TP-646**

Three layer zisha canisters in bamboo section design

H：24.7cm　W：12.7cm

刻字回紋紫砂茶葉罐　**TP-442**

Zisha teapot carved with Chinese characters

H：26cm　W：20cm

甕形刻字紫砂大茶葉罐　**TP-416**

Jug shaped zisha tea canister

H：38cm　W：33cm

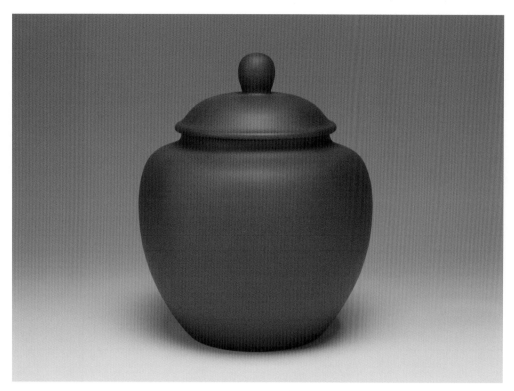

甕形紫砂茶葉罐　悟陶園製　**TP-437**

Jug shaped zisha tea canister

H：20cm　W：17cm

甕形紫砂大茶葉罐　**TP-417**

Large jug shaped zisha tea canister

H：42cm　W：39cm

桶形紫砂大茶葉罐　TP-415

Large zisha tea canister

H：31.5cm　W：27cm

六方刻字花草黃泥茶葉罐一對　TP-429

A pair of hexagonal yellow clay tea canister carved with flower design

H：17.5cm　W：12.5cm（左）

273

甕形山水彩茶葉罐　**TP-371**

Tea canister with landscape design

H：20cm　W：16.5cm

甕形龍紋黃泥茶葉罐　**TP-449**

民國二十年王元道定製

Yellow clay tea canister with dragon design,

Republican period

H：23.5cm　W：19.5cm

花草紋藍釉紫砂茶葉罐　**TP-452**

Zisha tea canister in blue enamel colors with flower design

H：13cm　W：14.5cm

藍釉紫砂茶葉罐　**TP-464**

Blue glaze zisha tea canister

H：21cm　W：18cm

壽紋雕花椰殼茶葉罐一對　**TP-484**

A pair of coconut shell tea canisters carved with flower design

H：14.5cm　W：12cm

珊瑚釉瓷茶罐　TP-468

Coral glaze tea canisters

H：12.5cm　W：11cm

珊瑚釉瓷茶罐　TP-469

Coral glaze tea canisters

H：12.5cm　W：11cm

六方粉彩瓷器茶葉罐　**TP-470**

Hexagonal tea canisters in famille rose enamel colors

H：14.5cm　W：10.2cm

鳳紋瓷甕茶葉罐一對　**TP-481**

A pair of porcelain tea canisters with phoenix design

H：9cm　W：7cm

貼花開片瓷茶葉罐　　TP-456

Porcelain tea canister in appligue design

H：18.5cm　W：20cm

青花瓷甕茶罐　　TP-458

Blue and white glaze tea canisters

H：12.5cm　W：14cm（左）

醬釉紫砂罐　**TP-453**

Brown glaze zisha tea canister

H：14.5cm　W：16cm

（左）水青釉紫砂罐　（右）黑釉紫砂罐　**TP-454**

L：Green glaze candy canister　R：Black glaze candy canister

H：14.5cm　W：15cm（左）

福字豆青瓷甕茶葉罐　**TP-461**

A celadon tea canister inscribed with
Chinese character "Fu"

H：21cm　W：21cm

TP-460

福字豆青瓷茶葉罐　乾隆御製

Celadon tea canister inscribed with Chinese
character "Fu" marked with "Qianong"

H：24cm　W：23.5cm

雙囍瓷茶葉罐　**TP-463**

Porcelain tea canister with
inscription of "Double happiness"
H：23cm　W：20cm

雙囍瓷茶葉罐　**TP-462**

Porcelain tea canister with
inscription of "Double happiness"
H：24cm　W：23.5cm

山水青花瓷甕茶葉罐　**TP-467**
Blue and while glaze tea canister
with landscape design
H：21cm　W：20cm

雙囍瓷甕茶葉罐　　**TP-465**
Porcelain tea canisters with inscription of
"Double happiness"
H：14.5cm　W：13.5cm（左）

青花瓷茶葉罐　**TP-455**

Blue and white porcelain tea canister

H：17.5cm　W：15cm

青花雙囍瓷茶葉罐　**TP-459**

Blue and white porcelain
tea canisters

H：24.5cm　W：22cm（大）

竹雕茶葉罐　**TP-427**

Bamboo carved tea canister

H：15.5cm　W：13cm

雲形錫大茶葉罐　　**TP-302**

Large cloud shaped pewter tea canister

H：48.5cm　W：35cm

太極錫茶葉罐　沈存周款　　　**JTP-744**

Pewter tea canister with the signature of Chen Chun Zhou

H：11cm　W：9cm

刻詩錫製茶葉罐一對　　沈存周款 **JTP-186**

A pair of flower pattern pewter tea canisters with the signature of Chen Cun Zhou

H：12cm　W：75cm

甕形錫製茶葉罐　沈存周款 **JTP-369**

Jug shaped pewter tea canister with the signature

of Chen Chun Zhou on the bottom

H：13cm　　W：10cm

甕形錫制茶葉罐　竹居主人刻款（沈存周） **JTP-367**

Jug shaped pewter tea canister with the signature of Chen Chun Zhou

H：7.5cm　W：8cm

JTP-204

甕形錫制茶葉罐

沈存周款

Pewter tea canister with the
signature of Chen Cun Zhou

H：11cm W：12cm

JTP-409

花瓣形錫制茶葉罐

沈存周制

Petal shaped pewter tea canister

H：10cm　W：5.5cm

JTP-368

四方錫制茶葉罐

沈存周款

Square pewter tea canister with signature of
Chen Chun Zhou on the bottom

H：8cm　W：4cm

JTP-365

鐘形錫制茶葉罐

沈存周款

Bell shaped pewter tea canister
marked by Chen Chun zhou

H：8cm　W：7cm

青花瓷錫蓋茶葉罐　沈存周款　**JTP-366**

Blue and white glaze tea canister with pewter lid and the
signature of Chen Chun Zhou on the bottom

H7：cm　W：11cm

巧木包錫茶葉罐　**JTP-375**

Nature wood wrapped pewter tea canister

H：10.5cm　W：12.5cm

巧木包錫茶葉罐　　JTP-378

Nature wood wrapped large pewter tea canisters

H：15cm　W：8cm（右）

巧木包錫茶葉罐　JTP-385

Nature wood wrapped large pewter tea canisters

H：13.5cm　W：9cm（左）

巧木包錫茶葉罐　JTP-381

Nature wood wrapped large pewter tea canisters

H：14cm　W：11cm（左）

巧木包錫茶葉罐　JTP-379

Nature wood wrapped large pewter tea canisters

H13.5cm　W14.5cm（左）

紫檀木包錫茶葉罐　**JTP-377**

Zitan wrapped pewter tea canisters

H：12.5cm　W：9.5cm（左）

巧木包錫茶葉罐　**JTP-380**

Nature wood wrapped pewter tea canisters

H：11cm　W：9cm（左）

巧木包錫茶葉罐 JTP-382

Nature wood wrapped pewter tea canisters

H：8cm　W：11cm（左）

巧木包錫茶葉罐　JTP-384

Nature wood wrapped pewter tea canisters

H：9.5cm　W：8.5cm（左）

竹包錫茶葉罐　**JTP-372**

Bamboo wrapped pewter tea canister

H：9.5cm　W：8.5cm

四方竹包錫茶葉罐　**JTP-373**

Square pewter cased bamboo tea canister

H：9cm　W：12.5cm

竹包錫茶葉罐　**JTP-387**

Bamboo and pewter tea canisters carved with flower patterns

H：9cm　W：7.5cm（左）

花瓣形木包錫茶葉罐　**JTP-383**

Petal shaped pewter tea canisters

H：11cm　W：11.5cm（左）

巧木包錫茶葉罐　**JTP-386**

Nature wood and pewter tea canisters

H：11cm　W：12.5cm（左）

貼花朱砂大碗　TP-649

Large red clay bowl in applique design

H：7.2cm　W：18.3cm

貼花朱砂碗　TP-581

Red clay bowl in applique design

H：5.5cm　W：11cm

紫砂綠釉大碗 **TP-648**

Large zisha bowl in green glaze

H：14cm　W：23.5cm

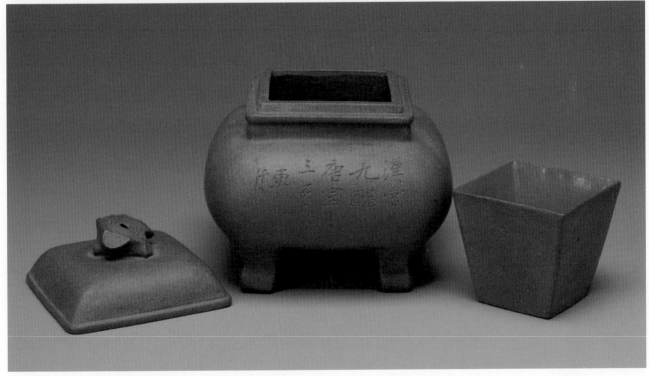

四足方形黃泥保溫杯組　**TP-573**

A set of square yellow clay tea cup warmer

H：9.7cm　W：9cm

鼓形紫砂保溫杯組一對　**TP-562**

A pair of drum shaped zisha tea cups warmer

H：8.4cm　W：8.5cm（左）

鐵畫軒茶杯組　　鐵畫軒製款　　　**JTP-466**

A set of tea cups with mark

H：3.5cm　W：7cm

紫砂白釉底茶杯組　**TP-619**

A set of zisha tea cups with white glaze

H：3.2cm　W：6.5cm

紫砂白釉底茶杯組　**TP-617**

A set of zisha tea cups with white glaze

H：3.3cm　W：6.3cm

心經四方紫砂杯一對　　**TP-599**

A pair of zisha tea cups inscribed of Chinese character "Xin Gen"

H：5cm　W：5cm

段泥白釉桃杯組　　**TP-606**

A set of peach shaped cups with white glaze

H：3.3cm　W：6.5cm

六方紫砂白釉茶杯組　**TP-618**

A set of hexagonal zisha teas cup with white glaze

H：3.3cm　W：6.5cm

紫砂白釉茶杯組　**TP-616**

A set of zisha tea cups with white glaze

H：3.3cm　W：6.2cm

粉彩瓷杯一對　　**TP-600**

A pair of porcelain cups in famille rose enamel colors

H：3cm　W：5.5cm

蝙蝠壽字瓷杯一對　　　**TP-596**

A pair of porcelain cups with bats and Chinese character "Longevity " design

H：3.8cm　W：6.5cm

粉彩瓷杯一對　TP-597

A pair of porcelain cups in famille rose enamel colors

H：4.3cm　W：7.5cm

黃釉竹紋瓷杯一對　TP-598

A pair of yellow glaze cups with bamboo patterns

H：5cm　W：7.5cm

粉彩瓷杯組　TP-607

A set of porcelain cups in famille rose enamel colors

H：3.5cm　W：6.5cm

雙囍瓷杯組　TP-608

A set of porcelain cups with inscribed "Double happinese"

H：3.9cm　W：6.5cm

青花若深瓷杯組　若深珍藏款　**TP-614**

A set of blue and white porcelain cups with mark

H：3cm　W：6.5cm

青花若深瓷杯組　若深珍藏款　**TP-615**

A set of blue and white porcelain cups with mark

H：3cm　W：6.8cm

青花蓋杯組 **TP-613**

A set of blue and white cups of lid with mark

H：6.5cm　W：9cm

青花杯茶具組　錦堂福紀款　**TP-295**

A set of blue and white glaze teapot and cups

H：4.2cm　W：12.5cm（左上）

青花蓋杯銀盤茶組　**TP-480**

A set of green glaze covered tea cups and silver plate

H：4.1cm　W：3.8cm（杯子）

椰殼銀茶杯一對 **TP-654**

A pair of coconut shell silver cups

H：3.3cm　W：5.7cm

椰殼銀茶杯一對 **TP-655**

A pair of coconut shell silver cups

H：2.4cm　W：6.3cm

椰殼包銀茶杯組　TP-601

A set of silver inlaid coconut shell tea cups　H：2.5cm　W：3.4cm

椰殼包銀茶杯組　TP-610

A set of silver inlaid coconut shell tea cups　H：5cm　W：8cm

椰殼包銀茶杯組　TP-612

A set of silver inlaid coconut shell tea cups　H：4.7cm　W：8.9cm

318

玉把四方錫包紫砂茶杯　石楳款　　**TP-602**

Square pewter cup of jade handle with mark

H：5cm　W：12.7cm

玉把錫茶盅　石楳銘款　　**TP-603**

Pewter tea canister of jade handle with mark

H：5.5cm　W：10.2cm

玉把錫茶杯一對　**TP-604**

A pair of pewter tea cups with jade handle

H：3.7cm　W：9cm

玉把錫茶杯組　**TP-605**

A set of pewter tea cups with jade handle

H：3.3cm　W：9.2cm（左）

魚紋白瓷杯　**TP-575**

White glaze tea cup with fish patterns

H：3.5cm　W：9.5cm

磁州窯茶碗　**TP-580**

Tea bowl

H：5.7cm　W：13cm

均釉瓷杯　**TP-576**

Porcelain cup in blue jun glaze

H：4cm　W：10.5cm

白瓷高燈杯一對　**TP-482**

A pair of white glaze cups

H：11.1cm　W：13cm

德化瓷杯　**TP-574**

Porcelain tea cup

H：3.5cm　W：7.5cm

醬釉瓷杯組　**TP-609**

A set of brown glaze porcelain cups

H：6cm　W：9.4cm

戰國繩紋茶杯一對　**TP-483**

A pair of tea cups with rob patterns, Warring States period

H：8cm　W：8.3cm

天目盤及窯坯　**TP-578**

"Jizhou" tea bowl and cup

H：13.5cm　W：19.5cm

玳斑天目碗　　**TP-486**

Tortoise shell glazed bowl

H：5.7cm　W：15.5cm

玳斑天目碗　　**TP-485**

Tortoise shell glazed bowl

H：5.6cm　W：15.5cm

魚紋天目碗　**TP-489**

Tea bowl ground in imitation of fish pattern

H：5.5cm　W：12cm

黑釉天目碗　**TP-490**

Black glazed tea bowl

H：5.5cm　W：12.5cm

建窯兔毫天目碗　　**TP-497**

"Jizhou" tea bowl ground in imitation of rabbit's motif

H：6cm　W：12.5cm

醬釉天目碗　**TP-493**

Brown glaze tea bowl

H：5.2cm　W：10.7cm

黑釉楓葉天目碗 **TP-488**

Maple shaped black glazed tea bowl

H：4.5cm　W：11.5cm

黑釉天目碗 **TP-495**

Black glazed plate

H：4.8cm　W：11.5cm

建窯天目碗　**TP-487**

"Jizhou" tea bowl

H：6cm　W：11cm

建窯天目碗　**TP-492**

"Jizhou" tea bowl

H：4.5cm　W：11.5cm

玳斑天目碗　　**TP-496**

Tortoise shell glazed bowl

H：5.5cm　W：10.5cm

玳斑天目碗　　**TP-494**

Tortoise shell glazed bowl

H：5.6cm　W：11.5cm

窯變天目碗　　**TP-491**

Tea bowl

H：5.5cm　W：11.5cm

藏式雕花銀製鑲銅奶茶壺　**TP-419**

Bronze inlaid silver teapot carved with flower design of Tibetan style

H：44cm　W：33cm

334

雕花銀制嵌銅奶茶壺　TP-418

Bronze inlaid silver teapot carved with flower design of Tibetan style

H：33.5cm　W：45.5cm

藏式雕花銀制奶茶壺　TP-420

Silver teapot carved with flower design of Tibetan style

H：24cm　W：27cm

 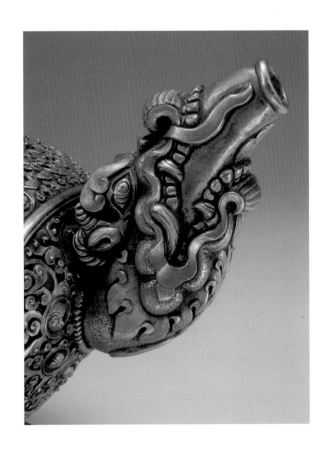

藏式銀製奶茶壺　**TP-422**

Silver teapot of Tibetan style

H：27cm　W：29.5cm

景泰藍提樑銀壺　**TP-433**

Cloisonne silver teapot with
overhead handle

H：21.5cm　W：19.5cm

337

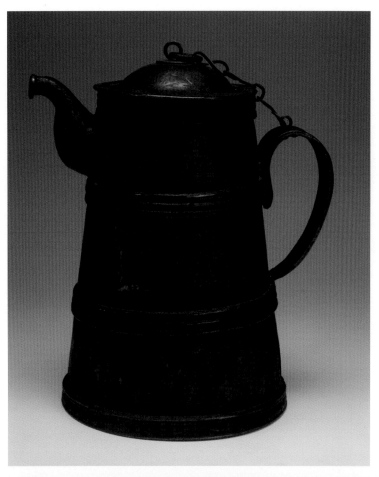

藏式銅製奶茶壺　**TP-421**

Bronze teapot of Tibetan style

H：22cm　W：19cm

藏式銅製奶茶壺　**TP-423**

Bronze teapot of Tibetan style

H：25.5cm　W：28cm

藏式陶製茶壺　　**TP-627**

Clay teapot of Tibetan style

H：18cm　W：20cm（左）＿

藏式陶製茶壺　　**TP-628**

Clay teapot of Tibetan style

H：28.5cm　W：21cm（左）

339

氂牛毛套碗　**TP-425**

Porcelain tea bowl

H：6.7cm　W：12.2cm

氂牛毛套碗　**TP-424**

Porcelain tea bowl

H：6.8cm　W：12.4cm

藏式青花茶碗組　**TP-625**

A set of tea cups in blue and white glaze of Tibetan style

H：6.5cm　W：12cm（左）

藏式粉彩茶碗組　**TP-624**

A set of tea cups in famille rose enamel colors of Tibetan style

H：6.5cm　W：13cm

藏式粉彩茶碗組　**TP-626**

A set of tea cups in famille rose enamel colors of Tibetan style

H：6.2cm　W：11cm

八吉祥供杯組　**TP-611**

A set of cups in eight auspicious emblems

H：4.8cm　W：9.5cm

宋白磁刻花壺　　　**JTP-653**

A white porcelain teapot of Sung Dynasty

H：9cm　　W：11cm

粉彩瓷器茶壺　　　　　　　TP-227

Porcelain teapot with famille rose enamel colors

H：13cm　W：16.5cm

粉彩瓷器茶壺　麟趾呈祥款　TP-301

Porcelain teapot in famille rose enamel colors

H：14.5cm　W：22cm

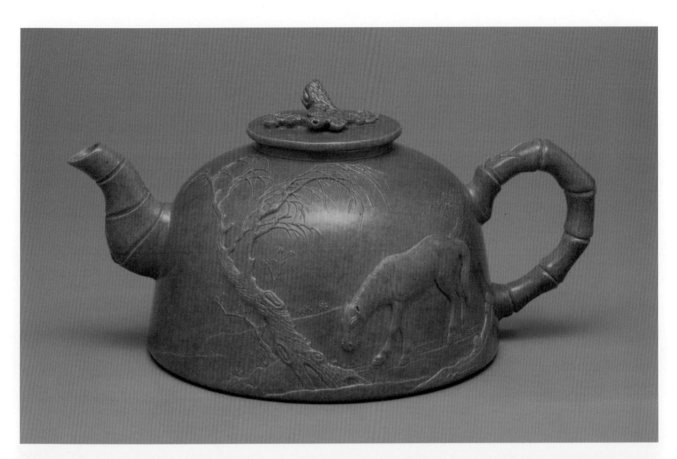

黃釉雕瓷壺　王炳榮款　TP-228

Porcelain teapot carved with yellow lacquer

H：7.5cm　W：16.5cm

梅幹金絲琺瑯銅茶壺　**TP-236**

Bronze teapot with prunes branch design in gold enamel

H：14.5cm　W：18cm

菊瓣蓋圓珠琺瑯銅茶壺　TP-235

Round bronze teapot in enamel with chrysanthemum petal lid

H：12cm　W：14.5cm

圓珠琺瑯銅茶壺　TP-234

Round teapot in enamel

H：12cm　W：15.5cm

稜形琺瑯銅茶壺　**TP-232**

Cloisonné inlaid bronze diamond shape teapot

H：13cm　　W：15cm

四方斜角琺瑯銅茶壺　**TP-233**

Square bronze teapot in enamel

H：16.5cm　　W：15.5cm

毛瓷彩繪茶具組　TP-290

A set of famille rose teapot and cups

H：18cm　W：21.5cm（茶壺）

毛瓷彩繪茶具組　TP-623

A set of teapot and cups, comtempory

H：17.5cm　W：21cm（茶壺）

白瓷套杯茶具組　TP-341

A set of white glaze teapot and cups

H：23cm　W：19cm

毛瓷彩繪茶具組　TP-622

A set of teapot and cups, comtempory

H：11cm　W：16.9cm（茶壺）

青花瓷提樑茶壺　　TP-255

Blue and white porcelain teapot with overhead handle

H：10cm　W：13.5cm

青花瓷提樑茶壺　　TP-229

Porcelain teapot in blue and white porcelain with overhead handle

H：14.5cm　W：15.5cm

巧雕描金玉茶壺　乾隆年製款　　**TP-348**

White jade teapot finely carved and gold burshed

Qing lung mark

H：8cm　W：11.5cm

巧雕白料茶壺　**TP-357**

Finely carved white glass teapot

H：13cm　W：27.5cm

巧雕白料茶壺　**TP-356**

Finely carved white glass teapot

H：17cm　W：31cm

石雕壺　廖天照款　**TP-130**

Carved stone teapot

H：11cm　W：17cm

石雕壺　天照石壺款　**TP-131**

Carved stone teapot

H：13.5cm　W：17cm

竹節形石雕壺　廖天照款　**TP-133**

Bamboo shaped stone carved teapot

H：6.5cm　W：10.5cm

石雕壺　石龍款　**TP-132**

Carved stone teapot

H：8.5cm　W：15cm

巧雕玉茶壺　**TP-354**

Finely carved jade teapot

H：11.5cm　W：15cm

巧雕玉茶壺　**TP-353**

Finely carved jade teapot

H：13.5cm　W：17cm

巧雕玉茶壺　**TP-346**

Finely carved jade teapot

H：12.5cm　W：19cm

巧雕玉茶壺　**TP-347**

Finely carved jade teapot with dragon design knob

H：14.5cm　W：16.5cm

水晶套杯茶具組　**TP-336**

A set of crystal teapot and cups

H：8cm　W：13.5cm（壺）

水晶套杯茶具組　**TP-414**

A set of crystal teapot and cups

H：12cm　W：16.5cm

左：菊瓣琥珀壺　右：壽桃琥珀壺　TP-386

Chrysanthemum petal shaped black jade teapot and Peach shaped black jade teapot

H：6.5cm　W：6.5cm（左）

巧雕玉茶壺　TP-355

Finely carved jade teapot

H：13cm　W：23cm

巧雕碧玉御壺　TP-349

Finely carved green jade teapot

H：7cm　W：12cm

巧雕碧玉御壺　TP-350

Finely carved green jade teapot

H：8.5cm　W：12.5cm

竹雕墨玉壺　**TP-351**

Black jade teapot carved of bamboo design

H：10cm　W：15.5cm

竹雕墨玉茶壺　**TP-352**

Black jade teapot carved of bamboo design

H：8.5cm　W：15cm

椰殼包錫圓珠壺　TP-071

Coconut shell teapot encased with pewter

H：10.5cm　W：19.5cm

椰殼包錫茶具組　TP-577

A set of coconut shell teapot and cups encased with pewter

H：12cm　W：21.5cm（右）

椰殼包錫提樑壺　**TP-072**

Coconut shell teapot with overhead handle encased in pewter

H：9.5cm　W：16cm

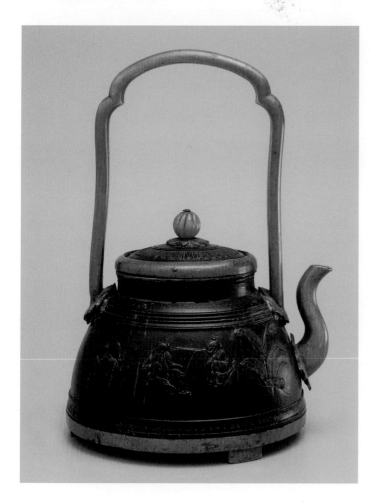

椰殼包錫提樑錫壺　**TP-030**

Coconut shell pewter teapot with overhead

handle encased in pewter

H：17cm　W：12cm

椰殼包錫提樑壺　TP-256

Coconut shell teapo encased in pewter with overhead handle

H：11cm　W：11.5cm

椰殼包錫茶壺　TP-652

Coconut shell teapot encased with pewter

H：13.5cm　W：21cm

雕龍銀製壺　**TP-231**

Silver teapot carved with dragon patterns

H：10cm　W：17cm

雕花銀製茶壺　**TP-620**

Silver teapot carved with flower design

H：9cm　W：13.3cm

台灣陶壺　**TP-298**

Ceramic teapot of Taiwanese style

H：18cm　W：25.5cm

台灣陶壺　**TP-300**

Clay teapot of Taiwanese style

H：20.5cm　W：25cm

台灣陶壺 **TP-297**

Ceramic teapot of Taiwanese style

H：23cm　W：22.5cm

青瓷提樑壺 **TP-291**

Green glaze teapot with overhead handle

H：37cm　W：28cm

醬釉水注 **TP-299**

Brown glaze ewer

H：23.5cm　W：22.5cm

青花瓷水注 **TP-292**

Blue and white glaze ewer

H：27cm　W：28cm

獻桃竹雕壺 **TP-368**

Finely carved peach shaped teapot

H：16cm　W：14cm

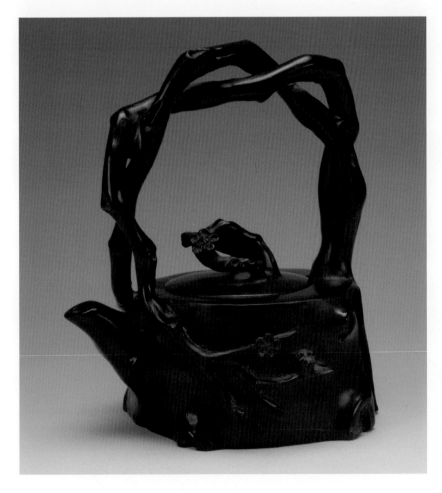

纏枝提樑石壺 **TP-244**

Stone teapot

with overhead handle

H：17cm　W：14.5cm

綠釉紫砂提樑壺　樂錦自製款　**TP-263**

Zisha teapot in green glaze with overhead handle

H：14.5cm　W：13cm

南瓜提樑陶壺　**TP-466**
何大均印款

Pumpkin shaped clay teapot
with overhead handle

H：33.5cm　W：32cm

TP-412

千兩茶柱一對

A pair of Pu-erh tea
of round pillar shape

H：147cm

W：27.5cm

　「千兩茶」原名花卷
茶，因一卷茶淨重一千
兩，故又稱千兩茶。過
去交通困難，茶葉運輸
不便，圓柱形的花卷茶
形如樹幹，便於捆在牲
口背的兩邊運送。零售
與飲用時則將千兩茶改
製成長方形的花磚茶。

茶磚顧名思義是將茶葉緊固成像磚的形狀，是緊壓茶的一種；一般用茶的枝梢製成黑茶、老青茶，或用綠茶、紅茶為原料，經蒸壓處理而做成磚頭狀。茶磚的飲用方式是「煮茶」或「熬茶」，先將磚茶敲下一部分搗碎，適量放入銅壺或鐵鍋中加水煮沸。《唐史》以「嗜食乳酪，不得茶以病」記載茶磚是藏族、蒙古族和維吾爾族生活中必須品，不可一日無茶的習慣；例如用茶磚製成的酥油茶是藏族每日必備的飲料，並已成為藏族飲食的代表飲品。

四川茯磚茶　　TP-402
Tea brick
L：37.5cm　　W：24.5cm

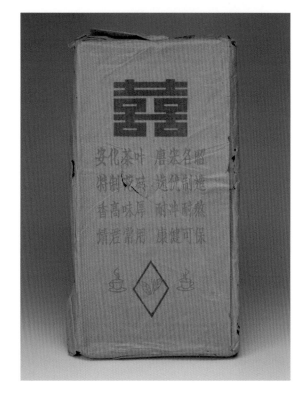

安化囍字特製花磚　　TP-642
Special make tea brick with inscription of "Double happiness"
L：35cm　　W：18cm

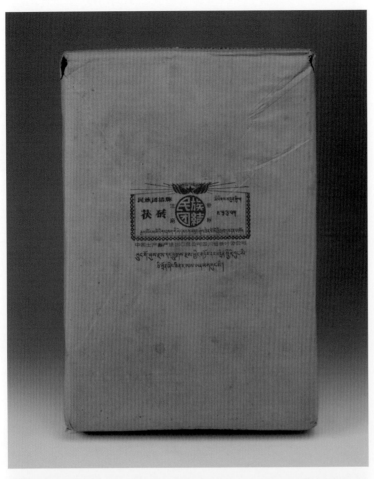

四川茯磚茶　　**TP-399**
Tea brick
L：37cm　　W：25cm

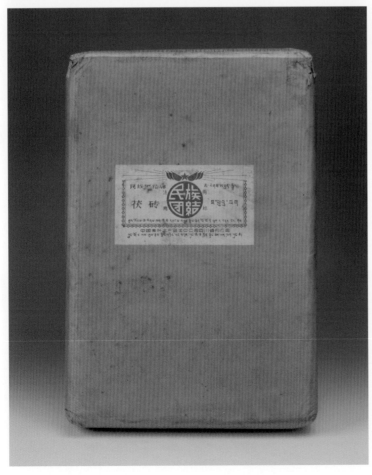

四川茯磚茶　　**TP-400**
Tea brick
L：36cm　　W：24.5cm

373

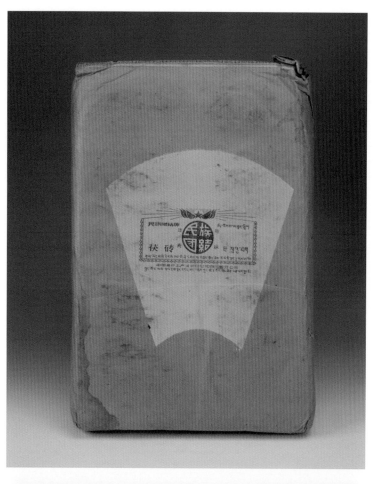

四川茯磚茶　　**TP-401**

Tea brick

L：37cm　W：25cm

廣西橫縣茯磚茶　　**TP-403**

Tea brick

L35cm　W19cm

犛牛皮套封存廣西橫縣大茶磚　　**TP-408**

Tea brick

L：73cm　W：40cm　H：270cm

犛牛皮套封存大茶磚　　**TP-410**

Tea brick

L：74cm　W：45cm　H：25cm

藏茶磚爲四川雅安地區生產的小葉種緊壓茶（屬黑茶類），此茶爲深度發酵茶，因含豐富的紅茶素，故湯色透紅，香氣純正，其口感不澀不苦，回味甘甜。尤其以包覆獸皮封存的陳年老藏茶，（因具有防潮、防蟲之功能）更是香味醇厚。

陳年老藏茶年代越久遠，自然的發酵力就越醇和，深具收藏的價值，近年有已有水漲船高之勢。

犛牛皮套封存大葉茶磚　TP-409
Tea brick
L：53cm　　W：48cm　　H：24cm

TP-405

犛牛皮封套存廣西壯族
梧州茶磚

Tea brick

L：55cm　W：45cm　H：18cm

TP-406

犛牛皮封套存滬牌茶磚

Tea brick

L：55cm　W：34cm　H：18cm

TP-407

犛牛皮套封存滬牌茶磚

Tea brick

L：55cm　W：38cm　H：20cm

犛牛皮套封存廣西壯族茶磚　**TP-404**

Tea brick

L：40cm　W：37cm　H：18cm

春芳民國早期外銷茶葉　**TP-411**

Early Republican age tea brick

L：49cm　W：41cm　H：57cm

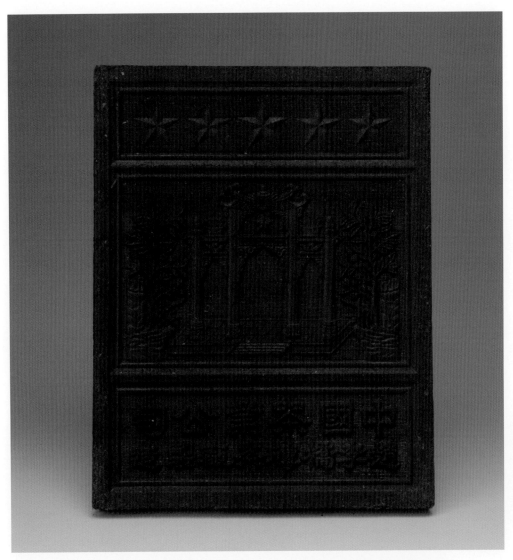

TP-636

五星門碑坊茶磚

Tea block

H：24cm

W：18.5cm

TP-645

可以興普洱方茶磚

Large Pu-erh tea brick

L14cm　W9.5cm

禧字茶磚　　**TP-633**

Tea brick with Chinese characters " Xi"

L：15cm　W：15cm

福祿壽禧茶磚　**TP-634**

Tea brick with Chinese characters

L：23cm　W：23cm

平西王府貢品陳年茶磚　　**TP-641**

Tea brick

L：29cm　W：19.5cm

TP-643

普洱茶磚

Large Pu-erh tea brick

made in 1949

L：29.5cm　W：19.5cm

TP-644

普洱茶磚

Large Pu-erh tea brick

made in 1958

L：30cm　W：20cm

TP-637

普洱茶磚

Large Pu-erh tea brick

made in1982

L：30cm　W：20cm

堯安號餅茶　　**TP-640**

Tea cake

直徑：21.5cm

香港回歸紀念餅茶　　**TP-638**

Transfer of the sovereignty of Hong
Kong tea cake

直徑：20cm

益字雲南七子餅茶　　**TP-639**

Tea cake

直徑：18.5cm

朱砂葫蘆塤　**TP-656**

萬曆壬寅大彬製

Red clay ewer with mark

H：12cm　W：7cm

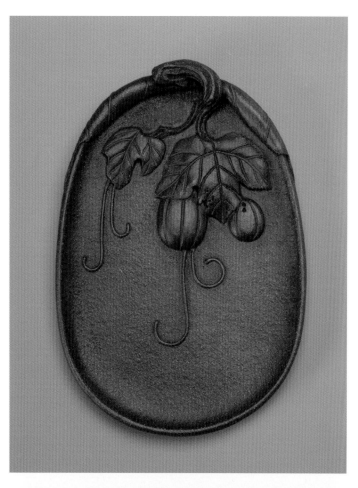

瓜形紫砂硯　　陳鳴遠款　**TP-678**
Melon shaped zisha inkstone
with Chen Mingyuan's signature
L：16.5cm　H：1.7cm

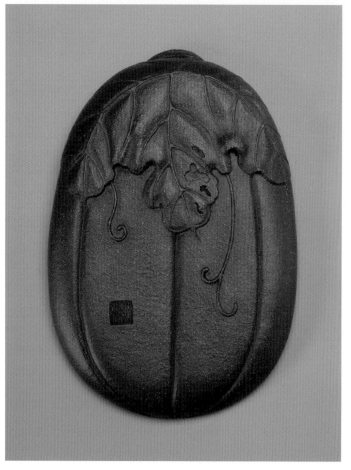

紫砂蓋罐　墨林堂大彬款　　**TP-668**

Zisha tea canister with mark

H：11.5cm　W：15cm

段泥印花圓盒　惠漢公製　**TP-669**

Blended clay round box in applique design

L：8.2cm　H：3.8cm

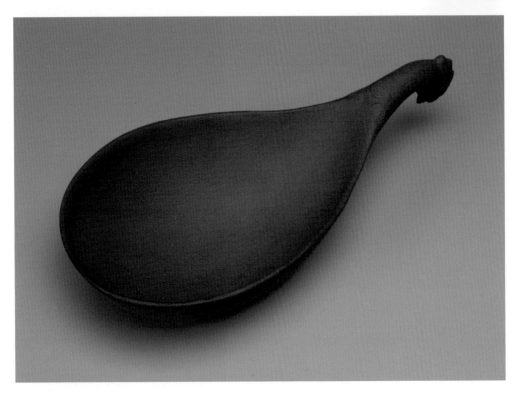

鳳首紫砂湯匙　**TP-666**

Zisha tea spoon with phoenix head decoration

L：16cm　H：4.5cm

桃幹朱泥杯　　**TP-589**

Red clay cup with peach tree branch design

H：6cm　　W：13cm

桃幹朱泥杯　**TP-142**

Red clay cup with peach tree branch design

H：8cm　W：15.5cm

紫砂聖桃杯　陳光明款　　**TP-684**

Peach shaped zisha cup with mark

H：6cm　　W：13.5cm

段泥煙灰缸　景舟款　**TP-681**
Blended clay ashtray with mark
L：11.8cm　W：7cm

紫砂葫蘆紙鎮　京次款　　**TP-689**

Calabash shaped zisha paperweight
with mark

H：10.5cm　W：4.5cm

紫砂貼花筆筒　陳子畦款　**TP-685**

Zisha pen holder in applique design with mark

H：11.5cm　W：9cm

紫砂小黃瓜擺件　陳鳴遠款　　**TP-682**

Zisha cucumber with Chen Mingyuan's signature

L：19cm　H：4.5cm

紫砂文房擺件　陳鳴遠款　**TP-688**

Zisha stationary sets with Chen Mingyuan's signature

L：14cm　H：5cm（左）

蟠螭紫砂水盂　**TP-686**

Zisha water container

H：11cm　W：13.5cm

菊瓣紫砂水盂　**TP-680**

Chrysanthemum petal shaped zisha water container

H：7.5cm　W：19.5cm

TP-660

堆泥紫砂筆筒　松壺款

Zisha pen holder in applique design
with mark

H：10.5cm　W：8.7cm

TP-673

朱泥花瓶　石仙款

Red clay vase with mark

H：12cm　W：7cm

三足紫砂花瓶　裴石民款

Zisha vase with three legs with mark

H：13cm　W：11.2cm

TP-659

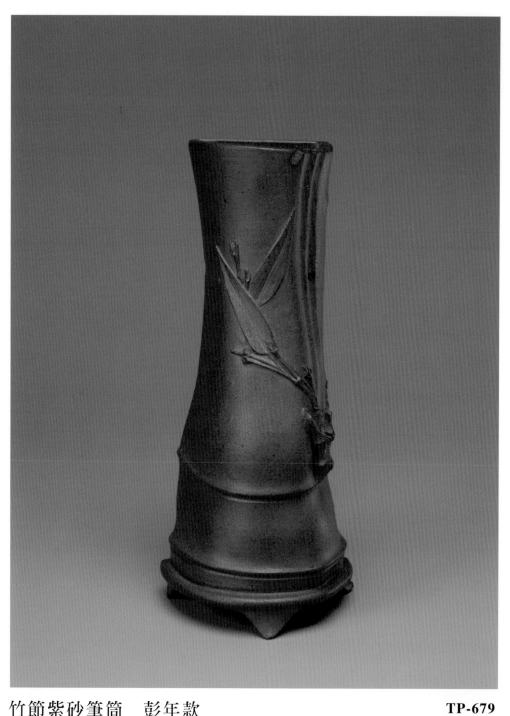

竹節紫砂筆筒　彭年款 **TP-679**

Bamboo shaped zisha penholder by Pengnian

H：16cm　W：6.8cm

樹椿黃泥筆筒

TP-651

Yellow clay pen holder in the shaped of tree trunk

H：16.5cm　W：12cm

樹椿段泥筆筒

Blended pen holder in the form of tree trunk with mark

H：14.5cm　　W：12cm

TP-664

段泥竹筍擺件　TP-670

Blended clay in bamboo shoot shaped

L：11cm　W：4cm

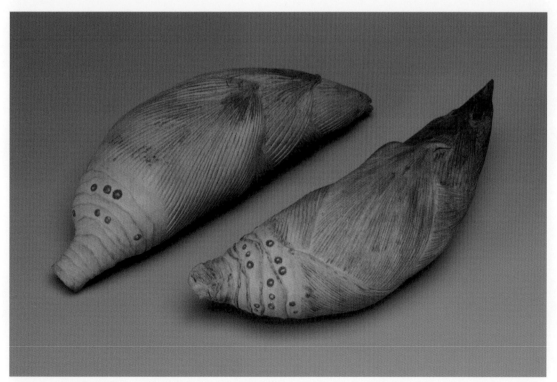

段泥竹筍擺件　玉芳款　　TP-667

Blended clay in bamboo shoot shaped with mark

L：15cm　W：4.5cm

田螺紫砂水盂　石民款　**TP-671**

Snail shaped zisha water container with mark

L：11cm　H：7.5cm

心經紫砂水盂　陳鼎和造款　　**TP-661**

Zisha water canister inscribed with Chinese character "Xin Gen"

L：10cm　H：5.5cm

枇杷段泥水滴　蔣蓉款　**TP-674**

Loquat shaped blended clay water dorpper

H：5.5cm　W：6cm

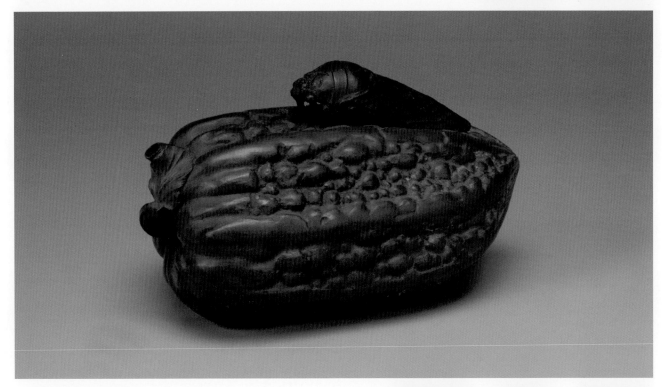

瓜形蟬鳴水滴　許四海款　**TP-658**

Melon shaped ewer with mark

L：14cm　W：7.5cm

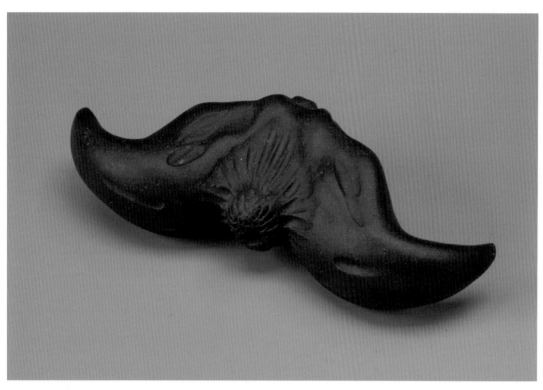

菱角紫砂擺件　蔣蓉款　**TP-676**

Zisha table ornament of a water caltrop shape

L：7cm　W：3cm

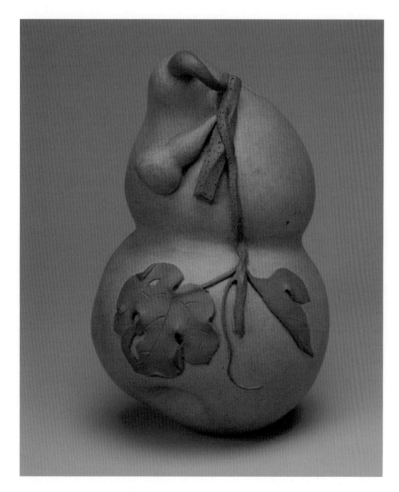

葫蘆段泥掛瓶　長星款　**TP-665**

Calabash shaped blended clay canister
with mark

L：15.5cm　H：6.5cm

龜形紫砂紙鎮　蔣蓉款　**TP-675**

Zisha turtle shaped paper weigh

L：9.5cm　W：7cm

龜形綠泥紙鎮　**TP-662**

Green glaze turtle shaped paper weigh

L：13.5cm　W：9cm

TP-693

荸薺紫砂把玩

Zisha water chestnut

H：3cm　W：3.2cm

TP-694

核桃段泥把玩

Zisha in walnut shape

H：3.2cm　W：3.2cm

TP-695

栗子紫砂把玩

Zisha chestnut

H：3cm　W：3cm

TP-692

洋荸薺段泥把玩

Zisha water chestnut

L：6.1cm　W：2.2cm

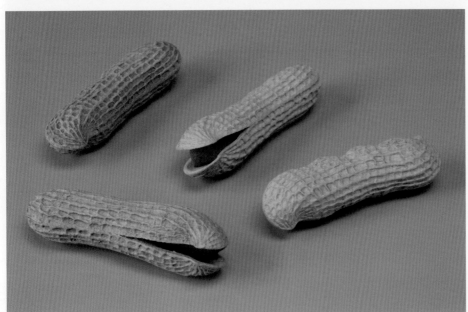

TP-691

花生段泥把玩

Blended clay peanut

L：4.7cm　W：1.4cm

TP-697

瓜子杏仁段泥把玩

Blended clay watermelon

seeds and almond

L：2.7cm　H：1.5cm

菱角紫砂把玩　**TP-696**

Zisha water caltrop

L：7cm　W：2.5cm

枇杷紫砂擺件　建芳款　**TP-683**

Zisha loquat table ornament with mark

L：13cm　H：5cm

紫砂水盂　蔣蓉款　**TP-657**

Zisha water canister

H：9cm　W：13cm

樹椿段泥臺面　蔣蓉款　**TP-677**

Blended clay tree trunk

L：13cm　H：4cm

佛手紫砂水盂　**TP-672**

Buddha's hand shaped Zisha water container

L：12cm　W：5.2cm

獅耳紫砂罐　**TP-539**

Zisha tea canister with lion shape handles

H：10cm　W：12.5cm

TP-434

葫蘆紫砂茶罐　朱新南制款
Calabash shaped zisha tea canister with mark
H：26.5cm　W：16.5cm

樹椿段泥筆筒　　　　　　　　　　　　　　　　**TP-650**

Blended clay pen holder in tree trunk shaped

H：28.7cm　W：15cm

獅耳藍釉紫砂四方對瓶　　　　　　　　**TP-647**

A pair of blue glazed square vases

H：21.5cm　W：9.5cm

獅紐蓋貼花紫砂香爐　　　　　　　　　　　　　　　　　　**TP-579**

A pair of zisha incense burner in applique design with lion shape lid

H：14cm　　W：19.5cm（大）

紫砂人物像　秀堂款　　**TP-663**

Zisha figure with mark

H：16.5cm　W：7.5cm

413

松幹虎頭蜂窩擺件

TP-413

A piece of beehive teunk

H：80cm　W：52cm

國家圖書館出版品預行編目資料

鬥品團香——王度中國茶文物珍藏展

Beyond the Fragrance and Fun : Chinese Tea-Wares and Tea Making Utensils from the
Wellington Wang Collection ╱王度著；國立歷史博物館編輯委員會編輯——

臺北市：史博館.民 96

428 面：29.7 公分

ISBN 978-986-01-0506-3(精裝)

974.024 960727-0001

鬥品團香——王度中國茶文物珍藏冊

Beyond the Fragrance and Fun : Chinese Tea-Wares and Tea Making Utensils from the Wellington Wang Collection

發 行 人	黃永川	Publisher	Huang Yung-Chuan
出 版 者	國立歷史博物館	Commissioner	National Museum of History
	臺北市 10066 南海路 49 號		49, Nan Hai Road,Taipei,Taiwan R.O.C.
	電話：886- 2- 23610270		Tel : 886-2-23610270
	傳眞：886- 2- 23610171		Fax: 886-2-23610171
	網站 : www.nmh.gov.tw		http:www.nmh.gov.tw
著 作 人	王度	Copyright Owner	Wellington Wang
編 輯	國立歷史博物館編輯委員會	Editorial Committee	Editorial Committee of National Museum of History
主 編	戈思明	Chief Editor	Jeff Ge
執行主編	溫玉珍	Executive Editor	Wen Yu-chen
編輯顧問	劉坤池、蘇子非	Consultant	Liu Kuen Chyr　Su Tzu-fei
助理編輯	王錦川、謝承佑、陳銘基	Assistance Editor	Wang Chin Chuan　Hsieh Chen-yu　Mickey Chen
翻 譯	林淪珊	Translator	Angie Lin
序文翻譯	萬象翻譯股份有限公司	Translator	Elite Translation Co. Ltd.
審 稿	孫素琴、潘信良	Proofreader	Jessie Wang　Pan Hsin Liang
攝 影	于志暉	Photographer	Yu Zhi-hui
總 務	許志榮	Chief General Affairs	Hsu Chih-Jung
會 計	劉營珠	Chief Accountant	Liu Ying-Chu
印 製	秉宜彩藝印製股份有限公司	Printing	BingYi Color Printing Co. Ltd.
出版日期	中華民國 96 年 8 月	Publication Date	August 2007
版 次	初版	Edition	First Edition
定 價	新台幣 3000 元	Price	NT$ 3000
展 售 處	國立歷史博物館文化服務處	Museum Shop	Cultural Service Department of
	臺北市 10066 南海路 49 號		National Museum of History
	電話：02-2361-0270		Tel : 02-2361-0270
經 銷 處	立時文化事業有限公司	Distributor	Harvest Cultural Enterprise Grorp
	電話：02-2345-1281		Tel : 02-2345-1281
統一編號	1009602068	GPN	1009602068
國際書號	978-986-01-0506-3	ISBN	978-986-01-0506-3